Leadership: Past, Present & Future

DR. HIRU BIJLANI

Copyright © 2024 Dr. Hiru Bijlani

All rights reserved.

ISBN: 9798334979840

DEDICATION

This book is dedicated to the hundreds of professionals that I have interacted with around the world in the 45 years of my consulting life.

CONTENTS

	Acknowledgements	viii
	Introduction	x
1	Leadership in Prehistoric Times	1
2	Leadership in Ancient Times	3
3	Leadership via Colonization	5
4	The Birth of Democracy and its Effect on Leadership	8
5	Various Theories of Leadership Styles Over the Last Century	13
6	Leadership is an Art & a Science	23
7	Leadership Styles	25
8	Becoming a Leader	34
9	Leadership Qualities Needed to Succeed	51
10	Feedback	59
11	Quotes and Lessons from Legends	65
12	Leadership in Politics	71
13	Leadership and Terrorism	75
14	Leadership and Corruption	77
15	Leadership and EQ	79

16	Leadership and Happiness	81
17	Leadership and Luck	83
18	Humour in Leadership	85
19	Personal and Professional Life of Leaders	87
20	Why Leaders Fail	91
21	Leadership Lessons from the Animal Kingdom	94
22	The New Psychology of Leadership	101
23	Emerging Leadership Challenges	109
24	Leadership Challenges and Solutions in Non-Profit Organizations	113
25	Future Challenges and Opportunities: The Way Forward	117
26	Applications of Behavioural Science and Technology	127
27	Leadership and Ethics	150
	References	156
	About the Author	178

LEADERSHIP: THE PAST, THE PRESENT, & THE FUTURE

ACKNOWLEDGEMENTS

I would like to extend my gratitude to Sharmin Karanjia for her editorial support, and to Ashok Thussu, my esteemed colleague and friend, for his invaluable professional insights and contributions to the content.

LEADERSHIP: THE PAST, THE PRESENT, & THE FUTURE

INTRODUCTION

Leadership is an important concept that has been studied and practiced throughout history. The past, present, and future of leadership can be viewed through several lenses, including the characteristics and traits of effective leaders, the role of leadership in society, and the challenges and opportunities facing leaders in a rapidly changing world.

In the past, leadership was often associated with a particular type of person, such as a king or queen, military commander, or religious figure. The focus was often on maintaining power and control, rather than empowering others or creating positive change. Over time, the concept of leadership evolved to include more democratic and participatory models, with an emphasis on collaboration, empathy, and service.

In the present, leadership continues to evolve, as organizations and societies grapple with complex challenges such as globalization, climate change, and social inequality. Effective leaders today must be able to adapt to changing circumstances, communicate effectively, build relationships, and inspire others to work towards a common goal. They must also be able to navigate the challenges of a rapidly changing technological landscape, and harness the power of new technologies to drive innovation and growth.

Looking to the future, the role of leadership is likely to become even more complex and challenging. As technological change accelerates, leaders must be able to adapt quickly and make informed decisions based on data and analysis. They must also be able to anticipate and respond to emerging trends and disruptions, and create a culture of continuous learning and innovation. Finally, effective leaders must be able to lead with purpose, inspiring others to work towards a shared vision of a better future for all.

LEADERSHIP: THE PAST, THE PRESENT, & THE FUTURE

PAST

LEADERSHIP: THE PAST, THE PRESENT, & THE FUTURE

1 LEADERSHIP IN PREHISTORIC TIMES

The evolution of human life spans about 7 million years. The need to create secure dwellings arose, and the caveman and woman were born. As the male human was biologically stronger than the woman, the man went out to hunt and foray for food. The woman stayed indoors in the cave to preserve the food and make forms of bodily warmth and protection from grass and leaves.

So, men and women played equally important roles, and both had leadership roles as equals. With the discovery of fire and the making of crude tools to fight adversaries and catch or kill food for consumption, came the competition amongst men for resources. Hence, man played a more dominant partner as he became not just the provider but the protector as well. From being solo hunters, during the ice age, the need for group comfort emerged. Thus, as humans evolved from apes first as hunters, they had to cope with challenges posed by the elements of nature, like the hot and cold weather, winds, sun, darkness, storms, etc. They also needed to cope with other species of life forms, hence human groups evolved.

As competing groups began to be formed with humans from other areas competing against other groups in a region, they began to cooperate to fend off other groups. The physically strongest of the group became the leader. Those in greatest need (whose food supplies dwindled first) to foray out and battle for survival, also emerged as the leaders of the group. So, besides being the strongest, the neediest emerged as leaders as they took the lead.

Thus, physical strength was the starting point of the claim to leadership – and continues to this day, be that muscular strength or nuclear strength!

The ability to survive in times of severe weather conditions, like extended winters, resulted in the need to gather food and store it for survival. Those who stored the most survived the longest. Thus, the requirements for survival over such conditions were a secure cave and stored food. The development of tools to optimize survival emerged.

Thereafter emerged human traits of empathy, mourning, and use of symbols (as beginnings of language), even today found in apes.

Factors of the beginnings of economic strength continue today and are increasingly evident in the trade wars and protectionism (yet while leveraging globalization) as the best possible forms of economic strength.

2 LEADERSHIP IN ANCIENT TIMES

With the beginnings of human forms of social life, power came from divine or mythical sources. Consider King Arthur and his sword Excalibur. Legends say that only one who was worthy could remove Excalibur from the stone it was stuck in, and was, thus, chosen by God to rule England. Many other ancient kings were said to be descendants of Gods or chosen by them.  At that time, people ruled because they happened to be born into families. Leaders who built bands and then armies of followers became the leaders. Orders were obeyed, usually because of the fear of punishment, in this lifetime or the next.

At this time, leaders were authoritarian, insulated from followers, demanding and dominating, expected unquestioning obedience, used fear to coerce their followers, and were rare. Only a few people were considered capable of being powerful leaders. Genghis Khan, for example, was among the noteworthy leaders of Mongolia who conquered most of Asia and Europe. His style of leadership could be classified as a combination of autocratic leadership and participative leadership. Genghis Khan was considered a dictator because the people he conquered were only given two options: either surrender to his will or be killed. However, when working with his army, he discussed his ideas and plans with them so that they could develop the best strategy for any given situation and enemy.

Autocratic leaders will rarely be able to maintain the goodwill and loyalty of their people for too long and will eventually encounter resistance from them, leading to internal conflict and eventual failure.

The leadership style of Alexander the Great of Greece was more participative and inspirational, as he shared his vision with his people to inspire them to achieve his goals as if they were their own.

Alexander had a certain set of principles. He would inspire his followers, ensure that each of them felt valuable, and would allow them to voice their opinions. He encouraged innovation and new ideas so that constant positive change was possible. He always had a clear vision and goal for every action that he took.

The Emperors of China and the Maharajas of India established unquestioning loyalty of their subjects, doing so by having loyal armies and local officials empowered and well paid and provided for. They collected taxes at will, and the territories conquered and ruled over had to obey or risk losing what they possessed, or even imprisonment or death. These leaders, at times, displayed benevolence on a whim towards their people; for instance, upon the birth of a royal child or during a patronaged festival. They lived lives of extreme luxury.

3 LEADERSHIP VIA COLONIZATION

With the discovery of the compass and gunpowder came the advent of seafaring. The colonization of countries commenced.

Leadership in that period was about conquest and exploitation using more advanced weapons than were available to the natives of these countries. Such conquests were often jointly done by enterprising seafarers, businesspersons, and the rulers of the countries.

Britain, France, Spain, Germany, and the Netherlands colonized countries in Asia, Africa and South America.

Raw materials, spices, and other goods were shipped from the colonies to parent countries/companies, enriching the ruler, owners of the factories, and conquering seafarers.

With the coming of the industrial revolution, where technology facilitated mass production of goods, there was a shift to urbanization of those people who lacked the land or means to cultivate it, taking up jobs that sprang up in factories, with people setting up home close to their place of work. Employers also saw an opportunity in getting their workers to work

longer hours by providing housing close to their factories.

The industrial revolution commenced sometime towards the end of the 17th century. Derbyshire in England with the first silk mill, Rolls Royce, and the railway engineering factory were founded. Before this, cottage industries were the norm with all work done by hand or handy tools and devices which were not mechanized. This was so until the invention of the electrical engine.

James Watt is credited with the introduction of systematic manufacturing processes for the production of engines. Eli Whitney introduced the manufacturing of interchangeable parts.

The Boston Manufacturing Company introduced the electric weaving looms for thread and cloth manufacturing in the early 18th century. The middle of the 18th century saw the beginning of modern management and leadership ideas by Daniel McCallum and Edgar Thomson in the railroad industry, with the designing of organization charts and the concept of staff and line functions.

The Singer Corporation, later known as the Singer Sewing Machine Company, in the middle of the 18th century, became the first company to go global. They had operations in Europe and South America to start with, and later, worldwide. At the same time, the Edison Electric Light Company was formed after Thomas Edison discovered the light bulb.

Towards the end of the 18th century, Frederick Taylor introduced the first modern management ideas of factory management techniques.

In the early 19th century, Henry Ford founded Ford Motors and the automobile industry was born. Mass production of interchangeable parts and assembly line manufacturing were introduced. Frederick Taylor published the book *Principles of Scientific Management* in 1911. Henry Gantt introduced the Gantt Chart for systematic project management techniques.

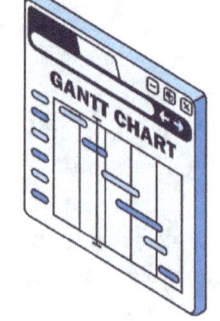

In 1919, Du Pont, another multinational, added chemicals and paints to its explosives manufacturing business as part of expansion and diversification.

A little later, Alfred Sloan of General Motors rationalized the creation of divisions in the automobile business by making cars of different sizes and prices for different markets.

Proctor and Gamble introduced the first ideas of mass marketing through branding and advertising boosts. They were focused on consumer products like soap, toothpaste, etc. Elton Mayo published *The Human Problems of Industrial Civilization* in 1933.

The creation of a category of executives who manage, as opposed to workers, was introduced by Chester Barnard in 1938 with his book *The Functions of Executives*.

In 1939, *The End Of The Economic Man* was published by Peter Drucker who dominated the ideas of modern management for the next 50 years.

4 THE BIRTH OF DEMOCRACY AND ITS EFFECT ON LEADERSHIP

In *The Social Contract*, published in 1762, Jean-Jacques Rousseau suggested that authority comes from the people who agree to give up some personal freedom in exchange for security and safety.

With the advent of democracy, power was transferred to elected representatives of the people via different democratic forms of government, such as a parliamentary or presidential form of government. Thus, power did not flow from God to the King but belonged to the people.

Once people began to choose their leaders, the leaders became accountable to them. Once leaders became accountable, people soon realized that those leaders can't always be trusted to do the right thing. So, checks and balances were introduced into the constitution of countries, and this has been an evolving process. This gave people the confidence to demand more respect and more autonomy from their leaders.

Abraham Lincoln was a great American leader. He wanted to serve his country and bring about positive changes that were revolutionary at the time, but he felt they would be beneficial for the country and its people in the long run. Abraham Lincoln had a servant leadership style. One of the vital components of this form of leadership is the importance of ethical values i.e., working for the benefit of the people. The servant leader wants to lead people because of a desire to serve them.

Abraham Lincoln's two greatest achievements were freeing the slaves and preservation of the Union of the United States – both of which had far-reaching effects long after his death. Mahatma Gandhi is among the most idolized personalities of most of the leaders worldwide, and many of them aspire to emulate aspects of his leadership style. Mahatma Gandhi embodied the servant style of leadership. He spent most of the second half of his life dedicated to India's  freedom struggle from the British. Gandhi revolutionized freedom struggles by focusing on non-violence even after being physically mistreated and imprisoned by the colonizers. He always encouraged his followers to focus on non-violent methods of protest. Gandhi had a clear vision about the independence of India and was able to communicate this vision effectively to diverse and dispersed people, by using simple and inspiring language and leading from the front. His moral and ethical standards were so high that people had implicit faith in him, almost to the point of considering him a saint. The strength and patience he demonstrated had made him a global icon. His non-violent freedom struggle eventually helped India gain independence in 1947.

 Nelson Mandela demonstrated an unbelievable attitude of forgiveness when he embraced the prison guard upon his release after serving 25 years of incarceration and hard labour on Robben Island in South Africa. He built a nation on forgiveness and created a rainbow nation of blacks, whites, and browns, without the bloodbath that happened in Rhodesia.

In this fast-paced modern world, leaders have to remain constantly vigilant for the many varied challenges that may arise and have to be prepared to deal with them in a calm and organized manner. Leaders of the 21st century need to be prepared for every contingency, developing processes and policies to deal with even the unlikeliest scenario.

PRESENT

LEADERSHIP: THE PAST, THE PRESENT, & THE FUTURE

5 VARIOUS THEORIES OF LEADERSHIP STYLES OVER THE LAST CENTURY

Leadership is a complex and diverse topic, and trying to make sense of leadership research can be an intimidating endeavour. There is a substantial scholarly body of leadership theory and research that continues to grow each year.

Given the sheer volume of leadership scholarship, readers must have some background knowledge of the history of leadership research, the various theoretical streams that have evolved over the years, and emerging issues. Further complicating the task is that more than one hundred years of leadership research have led to several paradigm shifts and a voluminous body of knowledge. Leadership researchers have struggled for most of the last century to put together an integrated, theoretically cohesive view of the nature of leadership, invariably leading to disappointment in those who attempted it. Also, the puzzle itself is changing.

Our accumulated knowledge now allows us to explain the nature (including the biological bases) of leadership, its antecedents, and consequences with some degree of confidence.

Leadership is a universal activity evident in humankind and in animal species. References to leadership are apparent throughout classical

Western and Eastern writings with a widespread belief that leadership is vital for effective organizational and societal functioning. Nonetheless, leadership is often easy to identify in practice but is difficult to define precisely.

Given the complex nature of leadership, a specific and widely accepted definition of leadership does not exist and might never be found. Fred Fiedler (1971), for example, noted:

"There are almost as many definitions of leadership as there are leadership theories—and there are almost as many theories of leadership as there are psychologists working in the field."

Most leadership scholars would likely agree, at least in principle, that leadership can be defined in terms of (a) an influencing process—and its resultant outcomes—that occurs between a leader and followers, and (b) how this influencing process is explained by the leader's dispositional characteristics and behaviours, follower perceptions and attributions of the leader, and the context in which the influencing process occurs. This is a multifaceted definition that is heavily "leader-centric" in describing mainly one-way effects associated with the personal characteristics of a leader. However, it also includes aspects of the interaction between leader and follower (in terms of perceptions and attributions) as well as a definition of leadership as an effect with regard to the resulting outcomes (e.g., goal achievement). Leadership is rooted in a context, which may affect the type of leadership that emerges and whether it will be effective. A broad definition of leadership thus incorporates the most commonly used definitional features: the leader as a person (dispositional characteristics), leader behaviour, the effects of a leader, the interaction process between a leader and follower(s), and the importance of context.

In setting forth any definition of leadership, it is also important to differentiate it conceptually from power and management, respectively, because these concepts are often confused with leadership. Power refers to the means leaders have to potentially influence others. Examples include referent power (i.e., followers' identification with the leader), expertise, the ability to reward or punish performance, and the formal power that is accorded legitimately based on one's role. Thus, the ability to lead others requires that one has power.

Regarding its distinction from management, leadership as seen from the "new" perspective is purpose-driven action that brings about change or transformation based on values, ideals, vision, symbols and emotional exchanges. Management is objective-driven, resulting in stability grounded in rationality, bureaucratic means, and the fulfilment of contractual obligations (i.e., transactions). Although some view leaders and managers as different sorts of individuals, others argue that successful leadership also requires successful management, that leadership and management are complementary, but that leadership goes beyond management, and that leadership is necessary for outcomes that exceed expectations.

At its essence, leadership is functional and necessary for a variety of reasons. On a supervisory level, leadership is required to complement organizational systems, establish and recognize group goals and values, recognize and integrate various individual styles and personalities in a group, maximize the use of group members' abilities, and help resolve problems and conflicts in a group. Thus, from a functional perspective, a leader is a "completer" who does or gets done whatever is not being adequately handled by a group. At the strategic level, leadership is necessary to ensure the coordinated functioning of the organization as it interacts with a dynamic external environment, i.e., the organization must adapt to its context. For this to occur, its leaders must monitor the external and internal environments, formulate a strategy based on the strengths and weaknesses of the organization and the opportunities presented by the environment, and monitor outcomes so that its strategic goals are met. Thus, leadership is required to direct and guide organizational and human resources toward the strategic objectives of the organization and ensure that organizational functions are aligned with the external environment.

Many different leadership schools of thought have emerged, such as those discussed below by various scholars.

Trait School of Leadership

The scientific study of leadership began at the turn of the 20th century with the trait-based perspective, which saw the shaping of history through the lens of exceptional individuals. This school of thought suggested that certain dispositional characteristics (i.e., stable personality attributes or traits) differentiated leaders from non-leaders. Thus, leadership researchers focused on identifying robust individual differences in personality traits that were thought to be associated with effective leadership. In two influential reviews, traits such as intelligence and dominance were identified as being associated with leadership. However, trait research, for most intents and purposes, was shut down following the rather pessimistic interpretations of these findings by many leadership scholars.

The Great Man theories focus on the subjective aspects of the individual leader himself/herself. According to this point of view, great

leaders are simply born with the necessary internal characteristics such as charisma, confidence, intelligence, and social skills that make them natural-born leaders. Great Man theories assume that leadership capacity is inherent — that great leaders are born and not made. These theories often portray great leaders as heroic, mythic, and destined to rise to leadership when needed. The term "Great Man" was used because, at the time, leadership was thought of primarily as a male quality, especially in terms of military leadership.

This was the first major crisis reorientation of leadership research, and it took almost 30 years for this line of research to re-emerge. The impetus for the re-emergence of the leadership trait theory came from a reanalysis of Mann's data using a relatively new and innovative analytic procedure at the time — meta-analysis. This analytic procedure proposed new ways of aggregating effects across studies to estimate effect sizes more accurately. The meta-analytic results offered by Lord et al. suggested that the trait of intelligence was strongly correlated ($r = .50$) with perceptions of leadership (i.e., emergence rather than effectiveness) and that this effect was robust across studies included in Mann's data as well as studies published after Mann. More recent meta-analyses confirmed that objectively measured intelligence correlates ($r = .33$) with leadership effectiveness as well (Judge, Colbert & Ilies, 2004). Studies by Kenny and Zaccaro (1983) and Zaccaro, Foti, and Kenny (1991) were also instrumental in demonstrating stable leader characteristics, such as traits related to leader emergence. David McClelland (1985), in the meantime, led another independent line of inquiry linking leader implicit motives (i.e., subconscious drives or wishes) to leader effectiveness.

There have been a few high-profile reviews of the trait perspective on leadership and particularly the moderately strong relationship of the big-five personality factors with leader emergence and effectiveness; however, there has been a decline in the proportion of articles published in The Leadership Quarterly (LQ) — a prominent specialty journal devoted to leadership theory and research. Research efforts in this area, however, shall probably continue as advances are made in psychometric testing and interest in other individual-differences areas (e.g., gender, diversity) increases.

Situational Theories

Situational theories propose that leaders choose the best course of action based on situational variables. Different styles of leadership may be more appropriate for certain types of decision-making. For example, in a situation where the leader is the most knowledgeable and experienced member of a group, an authoritarian style might be most appropriate. In other instances where group members are skilled experts, a democratic style would be more effective.

Participative Theories

Participative Leadership theories suggest that the ideal leadership style takes the input of others into account. These leaders encourage participation and contributions from group members and help group members feel more relevant and committed to the decision-making process. In participative theories, however, the leader retains the right to allow the input of others.

Transactional Theories

Transactional theories, focus on the role of supervision, organization, and group performance. These theories base leadership on a system of rewards and punishments. Managerial theories are often used in business. When employees are successful, they are rewarded; when they fail, they are reprimanded or punished.

Behavioural School of Leadership

The Ohio State and University of Michigan studies identified two overarching leadership factors generally referred to as consideration (i.e., supportive, person-oriented leadership) and initiating structure (i.e., directive, task-oriented leadership). Others extended this research to organization-level effects.

Nonetheless, leadership research found itself again in crisis because of contradictory findings relating behavioural "styles" of leadership to relevant outcomes. That is, there was no consistent evidence of a universally preferred leadership style across tasks or situations. From these inconsistent findings, it was proposed that the success of the leader's behavioural style must be contingent on the situation.

Contingency School of Leadership

The leadership contingency theory movement is credited in large part to Fiedler (1967, 1971), who stated that leader-member relations, task  structure, and the position power of the leader determine the effectiveness of the type of leadership exercised. Another well-known contingency approach was that of House (1971), who focused on the leader's role in clarifying paths to follower goals. Kerr and Jermier (1978) extended this line of research into the "substitutes-for-leadership" theory by focusing on the conditions where leadership is unnecessary as a result of factors such as follower capabilities, clear organizational systems, and routinized procedures. Other lines of research, presenting theories of leader decision-making style and various contingencies, include the work of Vroom and associates.

Relational School of Leadership

LMX theory describes the nature of the relations between leaders and their followers. High-quality relations between a leader and his or her followers (i.e., the "in group") are based on trust and mutual respect, whereas low-quality relations between a leader and his or her followers (i.e., the "out-group") are based on the fulfilment of contractual obligations. LMX  theory predicts that high-quality relations generate more positive leader outcomes than do lower-quality relations, which has been supported empirically. This line of research continues to find new directions, addressing various relational perspectives, including growing interest in the role of followers.

Sceptics-of-Leadership School

Leadership research faced yet another series of challenges in the 1970s and 1980s. The validity of questionnaire ratings of leadership was criticized as likely biased by the implicit leadership theories of those providing the ratings. This position suggests that what leaders do (i.e., leadership) is largely attributed based on performance outcomes and may reflect the implicit leadership theories that individuals carry "in their heads". That is, people attribute leadership as a way of explaining observed results, even if those results were due to factors outside of the leader's control.

In a related field of research, scholars argued that leader evaluations were based on the attributions that followers make in their quest to understand and assign causes to organizational outcomes. These researchers suggested that what leaders do might be largely irrelevant and that leader outcomes (i.e., the performance of the leader's group) affect how leaders are rated. Another related line of research questioned whether leadership existed at all or was even needed, thus questioning whether it made any difference to organizational performance.

Many of the above arguments have been addressed by leadership scholars who might be classified as realists rather than sceptics. Interest in the sceptics' perspective appears to have waned, although there is increasing interest in followers' roles in leadership processes. In addressing many of the questions posed by the sceptics' school, the study of leadership has benefited from (a) using more rigorous methodologies, (b) differentiating top-level leadership from supervisory leadership, and (c) focusing on followers and how they perceive reality. Furthermore, the study of followership and the resultant information-processing perspective of leadership have generated many theoretical advances that have strengthened the leadership field immensely.

Information-Processing School of Leadership

The major impetus for the information-processing perspective is based on the work of Lord and colleagues. The focus of the work has mostly been on understanding how and why a leader is legitimized (i.e., accorded influence) through the process of matching his or her characteristics (i.e., personality traits) with the prototypical expectations that followers have of a leader.

The information-processing perspective has also been extended to better understand how cognition is related to the enactment of various behaviours. Also notable are the links that have been made to other areas of leadership, for example, prototypes and their relation to various contextual factors. Information-processing perspectives of leadership have generated much attention, and the interest in leader/follower cognitions among contributors to LQ continues to grow. As a result, research in the areas of cognition, information processing, and emotions should continue to provide us with a novel understanding of

The New Leadership (Neo-Charismatic/ Transformational/ Visionary) School

At a time when leadership research was beginning to appear especially dull and lacking in any theoretical advances or insights, the work of Bass and his associates and others promoting visionary and charismatic leadership theories, reignited interest in leadership research in general and related schools of leadership (e.g., trait school).

Bass (1985) built on the work of Burns (1978), House (1977), and others to argue that previous paradigms of leadership were mainly transactional; that is, they were focused on the mutual satisfaction of transactional (i.e., social exchange) obligations. Bass believed that a different form of leadership was required to account for follower outcomes centred on a sense of purpose and an idealized mission. He referred to this type of leadership as transformational leadership, in which idealized and inspiring leader behaviours induced followers to transcend their interests for that of the greater good.

There are many ways of thinking about leadership, ranging from focusing on the personality traits of great leadership to emphasizing aspects of the situation that help determine how people lead. Like most things, leadership is a highly multi-faceted subject, and it is a mixture of many factors that help determine why some people become great leaders. Learning more about some of the things that make people strong leaders is one way of potentially improving skill sets.

Task-Oriented Approach

If your employees perform specific, repetitive tasks to achieve high productivity, the task-oriented approach is one of the most effective behavioural leadership examples you can adopt. With this approach, you focus on planning, coordinating, and

assigning tasks, and your managers assign those tasks based on the worker's skill set. This allows employees to feel as if they're being used based on their strengths, rather than being placed in positions in which they feel unsuited to the tasks required. By focusing on maximizing strengths and assigning tasks based on those strengths, this behavioural leadership example can help prevent employees from performing work that isn't a match for what they do best.

Needs-Based Approach

Managing your staff based on their primary needs is another behavioural approach example that can lead to success. In this approach, your managers must take into account the needs of their staff based on a hierarchical list developed by psychologist Abraham Maslow. In descending order, the list includes psychological, safety, belonging/love, esteem, and self-actualization needs. The behavioural approach example assumes that the driving motivation for most human beings is to satisfy some kind of need. Although it is impossible for people to fulfil everything they need, there must be a sense that some of those needs have been met. At work, managers can change workplace culture by doing their best to meet the most pressing of these needs. For example, if employee morale is low due to long work hours, a manager can offer more flexible work schedules to boost morale.

Path-Goal Theory Approach

In the path-goal behavioural approach example, the work environment and the characteristics of your staff influence which approach to take. The focus is on boosting employee motivation and empowering workers to do their best work based on a positive work environment.

There are four leadership styles under this approach: directive, achievement-oriented, participative, and supportive.

Under the directive style, a manager sets expectations and trusts employees to perform up to standard. The strength of this style lies in establishing expectations and providing employees with the resources to achieve them. Under the achievement-oriented style, managers set very high goals with the confidence that their employees can meet those goals. This style is often used in tech businesses, engineering, and science-based organizations. Under the participative style, managers solicit employee suggestions and ideas before establishing performance standards. This is especially useful in businesses such as content creation that require close collaboration to generate a quality product. Under the supportive style, managers are most concerned with the emotional and psychological health of their employees. Jobs that place a high level of emotional or physical stress on their employees benefit from the supportive style. For example, if you run a security guard business, you would use this style to ensure that your personnel receive counselling as a means of dealing with the after-effects of handling dangerous situations.

To develop leadership skills, a manager might use several different leadership styles at any given time. To fulfil the needs of the organization and the people working there.

6 LEADERSHIP IS AN ART AND A SCIENCE

Determining the nature and meaning of leadership leads us to the discussion of it being an art, a science or a bit of both. Our view of leadership depends on our perspective and the business environment.

Art allows for a more subjective interpretation of ideas or concepts, unlike science with its fixed answers and definitions. Art is not so much what the artist wants you to see as it is what you choose to see. From this point of view, it would seem leadership has characteristics of an art form requiring a leader to have the perception and intuition to see things that are not obvious to most people. However, one must also dissect the role of science in leadership.

Many scientific disciplines have helped us to understand the qualities of an effective leader. Developments in the fields of organizational psychology and neuroscience have helped us gain a better understanding of the traits a leader must have, and why they benefit the organizations and teams these individuals lead. Science may not be able to clearly define leadership, but it has proved to be vital to not only improving how we perceive this function but also how those who lead serve others through these roles.

However, a blind and singular scientific focus may be too simple to explain such a diverse activity. After all, a company, fundamentally, is a group of people. Companies don't have ideas; people do. Customers buy services or products created by people. CEOs worry about people a lot: getting the right ones, getting the best from them, inspiring them with the best projects and visions, etc. Their biggest challenge is getting their people to work well together. Dealing with employees and customers would require a leader to rely on more than just scientific metrics and case studies. Successful leaders need to be empathetic, intuitive and have the ability to inspire others.

Business schools mostly grew out of engineering schools. As a result, much of the language around management and leadership has a scientific tone. We talk about business models as though they really were engines that, with the right precise tinkering, could be persuaded to work. We search for connections between cause and effect that might provide the reassurance of physics. Orchestras, bands, quartets, and ensembles spend years working together to create the right sound and the best balance. The best filmmakers create a nucleus of people whose developed shorthand makes ever-richer projects spring to life. Even those artists we think of as soloists—whether Adele or Matisse—are, it turns out, highly dependent on the support, challenge, and inspiration they get from colleagues and competitors.

So, is leadership a definitive science or more of a subjective art form? It might be difficult and a bit unfair to label such a complex role in the narrow confines of an art form or a science. Its complexities demand the exactness of science as well as the perception and intuition of art.

7 LEADERSHIP STYLES

Coach

A coaching leader is someone who can quickly recognise their team members' strengths, weaknesses, and motivations to help each individual improve. This type of leader often assists team members in setting smart goals and then provides regular feedback with challenging projects to promote growth. They're skilled in setting clear expectations and creating a  positive, motivating environment. The coach leadership style is one of the most advantageous for employers as well as for the employees they manage.

Coaching leadership is most effective when leaders have the time to devote to individual employees. This style works best with employees who know their limitations and are open to change and challenges.

Visionary

Visionary leaders can drive progress by getting a buy-in to a vision, thus inspiring employees and earning trust for new ideas. A visionary leader is also able to establish a strong organizational bond.

This type of leadership is especially helpful for small, fast-growing organizations or larger organizations experiencing transformations or corporate restructuring, or challenging times and there is a need to build motivation.

Servant

Servant leaders put people first, especially their team. Because of their emphasis on employee satisfaction and collaboration, they tend to achieve higher levels of commitment. A servant leader is an excellent leadership style for organizations of any industry and size but is especially prevalent within non-profits. These types of leaders are exceptionally skilled in building employees.

Autocratic

Also called the authoritarian style of leadership, this type of leader is focused almost entirely on results and efficiency. They often make decisions alone or with a small, trusted group and expect employees to do exactly what they're asked. It can be helpful to think of these types of leaders as military commanders. They expect their team to be soldiers while they direct as generals.

This leadership style can be useful in organizations with strict guidelines or compliance-heavy industries. It can also be beneficial when used with employees who need a great deal of supervision such as those with little to no experience. However, this leadership style can stifle creativity and make employees feel confined.

Autocrats versus Nurtures

Amongst the big names, the contrast between Bill Gates and Steve Jobs is striking. Gates has a nurturing, delegating style with a focus on encouraging innovation and empowerment and sharing information and is willing to risk expensive mistakes.

Steve Jobs, in contrast, dazzled his teams by dint of his personality, with his creativity and personal hands-on involvement in the business, especially focusing on being ahead in the application of technology race. Yet, his Macintosh lost out to Gates' Windows. He rose again from the ashes, by dint of his hard-working style, where everyone in his organization worked up to 14 to 16 hours as he did personally, and focused on technology and took a good bet on the emergence of the cell phone, building the iPhone brands and Apple computers. His was an autocratic style, and he never hesitated to hire and fire. Such examples of leaders being successful are rare.

Laissez-Faire or Hands-Off

This leadership style is the opposite of the autocratic leadership type focusing mostly on delegating many tasks to team members and providing little to no supervision. Because laissez-faire leaders do not spend their time closely managing employees, they jointly set goals and periodically review results. This style works when team members are  experienced, well-trained, and require little oversight. It's also useful in situations when trusted employees engage in individual projects or when creative tasks or problems require out-of-the-box thinking.

Democratic

Democratic leaders ask for input and consider feedback from their team before making a decision. Because team members feel that their voice is heard and their contributions matter, a democratic leadership style is often credited with fostering higher levels of employee engagement and workplace satisfaction. This type of leadership drives discussion and participation, it's an excellent style for organizations focused on creativity and innovation such as those in the technology industries.

Democratic leadership is most effective when you have the time to thoroughly assess processes and figure out ways to achieve long-term ideas and goals. It can be highly effective in companies – and for tasks – that benefit from creativity and inspiration.

Affiliative

Affiliative leaders, also known as facilitative leaders, aim to put employees first. They pay close attention to and support the emotional and professional needs of employees. Ultimately, this style focuses on

encouraging harmony and forming peaceful, collaborative relationships within teams. Most decisions are left to employees, but the leader is still part of the decision-making process. Affiliative leaders often use praise and helpfulness to build individual and team-wide confidence.

Affiliative leadership is most effective when morale is very low or there are conflicts among team members. Affiliative leadership can also be helpful during times of high stress, for example during unusually busy or short-staffed seasons. Affiliative leaders must have strong communication skills and be able to address conflict in a level-headed manner.

Pacesetter

The pacesetting leaders work 24x7 and are hard taskmasters. These leaders are primarily focused on performance. They often set high standards and hold their team members accountable for hitting their goals. They hire and fire easily. They do not encourage too much creativity or feedback. Pacesetting leadership is most effective when working with highly motivated employees who also like to move and see results quickly. It's a great  style of leadership for when a crucial deadline must be met, especially in a production or manufacturing environment.

Transformational

The transformational leader looks for, inspires, and drives big change in the way the organization is run and managed. They encourage their teams to do likewise. They tend to set objectives by mapping out where the company is going and what will happen when they get there. This inspired, future-focused vision is used to set expectations that engage and energize employees.

Transformational leaders might also encourage – and empower –

team members to step out of their comfort zones in the name of professional development and organizational achievement. Employees may be asked to share input on how to achieve common goals.

Transformational leadership is most effective in fast-growing organizations or organizations that have been drifting and need direction. Because these types of leaders spend much of their time on the big picture, this style of leading is best for teams that can handle many delegated tasks without constant supervision. Transformational leadership is also effective during corporate restructuring, mergers and acquisitions, and other high-risk business transformations.

Transactional

A transactional leader is someone who is laser-focused on performance similar to a pacesetter. Under this leadership style, the manager establishes predetermined incentives usually in the form of monetary reward for success and disciplinary action for failure. Unlike the pacesetter leadership style, transactional leaders are also focused on mentorship, instruction, and training to achieve goals and enjoy the rewards.

Bureaucratic

Bureaucratic leaders expect their team members to follow the rules and procedures where each employee has a set list of responsibilities and there is little need for collaboration and creativity. This leadership style is most effective in highly regulated industries or departments such as the armed forces or government.

One can select the relevant leadership style for the situation or flex style i.e., using different styles as needed.

The Leader as a Facilitator

In an environment of rapid change, no single person can know all, see all, and do all. Command and control styles of leadership under these conditions break down and are ineffective. Junior managers on the front lines have the information they need to respond to changes rapidly, but they must be given the authority and tools they need to act.

LEADERSHIP: THE PAST, THE PRESENT, & THE FUTURE

Historically, "leadership" has largely been considered a top-down function. Leaders were masters of their crafts and doled out their knowledge over time to eager apprentices aspiring to gain wisdom. Then as time passed and the average levels of education began to rise, workers began to know more about what they were doing than their boss, Peter Drucker called these workers, the "Knowledge Workers".

Fundamentally, the ever-increasing presence of the Knowledge Workers threatens to render our traditional assumptions about top-down leadership obsolete. It also presents challenges to modern-day leaders that their counterparts in years gone by were not called to address: How do you help your team members achieve their goals when you – as a leader – are not an expert on the topic?

To illustrate these challenges, we will examine how one CEO, Alan Mulally, gained well-deserved notoriety for creatively leveraging the skills of his team, the people of the Ford Motor Company, and the Situational Leadership® Model to lead an incredibly successful turnaround. This example demonstrates how "The Leader as Facilitator" has a higher probability of success than "The Leader as Boss" when leading Knowledge Workers.

When Alan assumed the role of CEO in 2006, here are a few of the top-line challenges that awaited him:
1. Ford had just posted the largest annual loss in its 103-year history
2. The stock was trading at $1 per share
3. Employees were paralyzed with fear

Alan's first acts were to form a cohesive leadership team and come together around a compelling vision, comprehensive strategy, and relentless implementation process. He then convened a weekly meeting with the 16 members of his leadership team (all of whom would certainly fit the definition of a Knowledge Worker). Initially, Alan asked each of them to do two things:
1. Identify a plan to implement the strategy
2. Assess progress against the plan using the following guidelines:
    a) GREEN – On plan, currently on target and projected to achieve goal
    b) YELLOW – Not currently on plan, but trending in a direction that would ultimately deliver desired results
    c) RED – Not on plan, and not sure how to get there.

Each of the 16 team members reported GREEN (even though their company was headed toward a record $17 billion loss). In light of the impending reality, Alan encouraged his team to try it again. After some time, Mark Fields finally said, "RED!" He then went on to candidly describe a problem of significance with no real strategy to fix it.

Looking back, Alan viewed this as one of the most important moments in the turnaround of Ford. In response to Mark's transparent assessment, Alan stood up and applauded. He congratulated Mark on having the courage to openly admit he had a problem and even more to admit that he had no idea on how to solve it, but that he was working on it.

He then said something few leaders have the nerve to say in the presence of their leadership teams. Alan said that he didn't have an answer to Mark's problem either but that they had thousands of very smart people working at Ford so they needed to find someone who could help Mark.

The team immediately focused on Mark's problem and identified people who had the experience and expertise to help. Within a few minutes, they were all moving in a positive direction. What followed was a series of bold and effective decisions that drove a truly legendary transformation. Alan retired in 2013 and during that year, Ford earned $7.2 billion, which translated to record profit-sharing bonuses of approximately $9,000 per employee.

Several lessons from Alan's experience at Ford are transferable to anyone tasked with the responsibility of leading Knowledge Workers:

1. Target transparency and applaud when you get it – Most of us have difficulty articulating our struggles in a public forum, especially in the presence of our superiors and peers. This probably stems from old-fashioned managers who asked for solutions and did not want to hear about their team's problems. That is exactly the opposite of what an effective leader should want. If people have problems, you want to get them out in the open so you can help solve them. When Mark Fields said,  "RED," Alan went out of his way to say, "That's OK," and provided the kind of positive recognition that encouraged truth and inspired trust.
2. Recognize that knowledge is power – Leading a Knowledge Worker

 means they know more than you do. Embracing that reality in the context of organizational power is critical. Managers can rarely force people to tell them the truth. They can, however, create a forum where truth-telling is celebrated, rewarded, and normal.

3. Be wary of making suggestions without true expertise – It is difficult for the formal leader to make suggestions. If Alan had just tried to tell Mark what to do, there would have been a strong tendency for Mark to focus on implementation. This is problematic for two reasons:
   a) It may well have been a sub-optimal suggestion by a leader with insufficient knowledge.
   b) There would have been limited to no personal ownership moving forward from anyone on the team since they were just following their leader's orders. After hearing "RED" and providing recognition for the honesty, Alan made it clear that he would not be the source of a solution. It may seem odd, but this more than anything was a call to collaborative action.

4. Actively involve others – If the problems Ford was facing when Alan became CEO were well-defined and simple, somebody would have solved them long before he arrived. Ford faced monumental and highly complex challenges. Almost immediately, Alan called upon the collective wisdom of the "thousands of very smart people" at Ford to help solve them. It is in this light that the  "Leader as Facilitator" is distinguished from the "Leader as Boss." Alan leveraged the legitimacy of his position as the driving force behind the search for solutions he was incapable of producing based on his experience alone.

5. Check your ego at the door – Fundamentally, leading Knowledge Workers requires that the leader get rid of ego and focus on achievement. Again, to quote Peter Drucker, *"Our mission is to make a positive difference, not to prove how smart we are."* The first step in responding to a challenge occurs when team members are willing to admit a challenge exists. The second step in addressing the challenge occurs when leaders are willing to admit they don't have all the

answers and facilitate the process of finding solutions.

With ever-increasing regularity, leaders at all levels in organizations will be responsible for effectively influencing Knowledge Workers. Creating an environment where those individuals can transparently communicate their level of performance provides the leader with the opportunity to facilitate forward movement, accomplish important goals, and build a culture that thrives on achievement.

A leader's transition from boss to facilitator is a function of the leader's ability to create an open and transparent environment that encourages team members to assess and articulate their level of performance without fear or shame of any kind and be open to help from people at any level of the company.

Developing One's Own Leadership Style

Leadership style is grounded in our personal preferences, which can be difficult to change. However, understanding your natural leadership style – and knowing when other styles can be more effective – can help you expand your skillset and become a better leader.

Tips for Developing Your Leadership Style:

1. Know yourself – start by learning your dominant leadership style. Do you prefer to give orders or delegate authority? Or do your preferences lie somewhere in between? Ask trusted colleagues to describe your leadership strengths and/or take a leadership assessment.
2. Know your employees – your leadership style is directly related to how you communicate with your team. It's important to adapt to employees' personalities and specific project-related circumstances. For example, you may be able to take a delegative leadership approach with team members who thrive doing autonomous work, whereas an autocratic approach may benefit new employees or individuals who prefer having clear directions to follow.
3. Know the leadership styles – familiarize yourself with the continuum of common leadership styles and focus on which may work best for different situations relevant to you and your business. What new skills might you need to develop? For example, if you tend to be a pacesetter, it might be smart to work on some affiliative leadership skills to help prevent employee burnout. Identify new skill sets and work to incorporate them into your leadership approach.

8 BECOMING A LEADER

Everyone can be a leader. Many of us already lead a family, group, or team of some sort, and we can of course be leaders through our ideas and influence, besides being a boss in a formal hierarchy.

A leader is someone whom people tend to follow. To command a following – a willing following – the leader has to do something, or be something, that makes people follow. There has to be something that inspires trust, respect, or admiration. That "something" must appeal to the creative, intuitive right brain as well as the logical.

It is the thinking and attitude behind behaviour that prove to be the critical differences – the differences that give the leaders a special edge. The leader is a thinker. Leaders are imaginative, intuitive, perceptive, and creative, producing quality ideas, as well as hunches, insights, and the 'Eurekas', or flashes of inspiration that seem so different from ordinary, deliberate thinking. Right–brain thinking traits are more or less universal among the top leaders.

As well as thinking in this bicameral way, leaders seem to know where they are going in both a personal and a business sense. They are quite happy with the goals and objectives. But these form part of widely differing thinking styles and motivate the leader in different ways. There is an interesting personality model that places goals in the categories of knowing, having or getting, doing, relating (to people), and being. These are termed 'life contents'. Each of these tendencies becomes apparent when we examine how different people achieve their personal or business goals. For example, some people are concerned with acquiring things (getting/having), while others want action – to have a go (doing). Some like to get as much information (knowing) as possible before they act, using knowledge as a form of power. In other cases, relationships are uppermost; the consideration being what will others think or do. But the "being" category is rather special, in that our desire to know, do, have, or relate is usually towards the end of being – being financially secure, being comfortable, being respected, being happy, and so on. This fundamental desire to be is invariably central to any study of human excellence, and leadership is no exception.

Having clarity of vision is an important starting point for good leadership. "Without a vision", says the Old Testament, "the people perish". This wisdom (that long predates business schools) links in with our clearer understanding of the human mind and the nature of "inner vision". The role of a visionary can make a manager a leader.

The visionary is more than a visualizer, although using the same mental skills. Vision looks ahead, not just around. And the long-term direction of a company is firmly the responsibility of its leader whose skill is in visualising – not just remembering faces, but creating a future, a dream, big enough and clear enough for others to follow.

Vision is very personal – it happens inside the head and the heart. A strong vision guides, or perhaps drives, the leader in just about everything he or she does. It will inevitably give a leader the edge over the manager who tends to take a short-term view of things, and who is motivated more by outside factors than an inner vision. As a thinking skill, envisioning gives the leader an advantage. The leader's dream – another word with its connotations – gives direction and motivation when others seem to be overwhelmed by events and circumstances.

A vision can sometimes be hard to communicate and initially unlikely to be supported by arguments, analysis, or the "facts" of a situation. As a right brain creation, it may not be easily communicated in the left-brain terms of language and logic.

Sir Keith Bright, former chairman of Brent Walker, had a "dream" about growth in the Far East market that could not have been supported by any rational extrapolation of earlier performance or equated with what competitors had achieved in a given timescale in that area. But his description of events contained a significant statement. As he put it: "I began to believe it". This belief, that accompanies a true vision as distinct from either wishful thinking or merely written plans, seems to be what correlates with eventual success. Belief grows as the vision becomes clearer. And the vision in turn becomes clearer. The picture inside takes on a clarity that is close to reality. For the visionary, it is experienced, so it has to be possible. It is believed, even though it is not yet known how it will be accomplished, or how the many obstacles in its path will be removed.

Vision belongs to the soft, mystical side of management and sits uncomfortably with the doing, macho part of a modern manager's armoury. It has to do with how we think; how we use the mind, and specifically the natural visualizing skill we all have to some extent. For this reason, vision rarely appears in a management job description, although it suddenly becomes a key issue when you reach the number one position. Vision concerns not the analytical side of our thinking, but the part that is concerned with imagination, intuition, and creativity. It consists of images, rather than words, numbers, and abstractions.

Fortunately, we have learned a lot from neurophysiology about these different modes of thought, carried out on the two sides of the brain. In calling on visionary powers, the leader becomes a right-brain thinker – able to imagine scenarios that as yet do not exist, able to make mental pictures of otherwise abstract goals. In a quite literal sense, he can experience subjectively (seeing, hearing, and feeling inwardly) something before it has become reality objectively.

Some Ideas on Envisioning for Becoming a Great Leader

Picture yourself excelling in these situations, whilst daydreaming or before going to sleep at night. Think about how you feel. Do you get frequent flashes of inspiration? Do you have to feel right about the decision? Or does everything have to stack up logically? This self-awareness is an important start to tapping into your leadership skills.

Determine your "life contents". You can

easily put your goals into categories (knowing, doing, getting/having, relating, being) by the words you use: "I'd like to have", "I'd like to be", etc. You can also change their relative importance. This is the inner you and you can always change what's inside.

Think further about how you feel. Do you like to think in pictures – visually – or are you an auditory (hearing), kinaesthetic (feeling) sort of person? Do you, for example, find it easier to remember people's faces than their names? Start using inner senses you are not so familiar with when exploring memories and anticipating forthcoming events.

Start developing an inner vision about where you want to be and what you want to do. Repeat and clarify your inner vision until it becomes very real. Check that it does not conflict with other goals you have and amend your desires so that there is harmony in different parts of your life. See yourself as a leader, and at home as well as at work – you are changing who you are, not just your job role.

Start using your thinking powers in everyday situations. When hiring staff, imagine them in the different roles they will have to play. If reorganizing an office system, visualise clearly what things will eventually look like. Incorporate these thinking skills into every part of your life and work.

Practise also long-term visioning – perhaps a dream holiday or a couple of jobs ahead, or retirement. This is a learned skill, not a  leadership trade secret. More than anything, the leader has to bring creative thought to bear fresh ideas in seemingly ordinary situations. Keeping in touch can be extended to visits to competitors having similar multiple outlets or plants. To avoid the activity being seen as "corporate tourism", the teams involved presented what they had learned to other staff soon after getting back to the company.

Much of the vital work of the mind happens below the level of consciousness and is not helped by trying. So, whilst seeming to expend much effort, a rational, logical, cerebral manager may not produce the results that a more natural leader, thinking holistically, produces.

The various occasions when creative "quality" thinking occurred, were associated with relaxing times. You can simply treat times when you relax as opportunities to think, solve problems, and come up with good ideas.

Most of the examples of what appeared to be right-brain creative thinking quoted by leaders seemed to take place at times when they were either on their own or at least had a measure of "private space". Many listed private spaces as linked with self-understanding. So, for example, sitting anonymously in a hotel lounge or an airport would qualify, as would a car or train journey. This explains why the office itself can be so sterile, as it usually affords little privacy.

Thinking about tests highlights the importance of both sides of the brain operating separately, each with its unique way of "thinking", but at the same time, the importance of both sides working together, to "make up our mind".

Thinking like a leader means using more of the whole mind. You need to keep every ounce of logic, rationale, prudence, and professionalism, with financial awareness or some solid functional training. Quick fix, ad hoc style is hardly workable in large organizations. This may be ok for start-ups in the early stages.

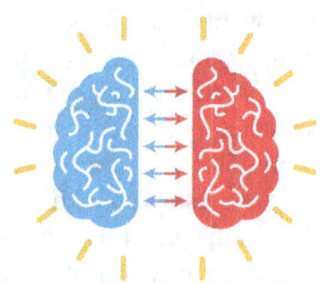

Leadership And Passion

It is often said, "When there is no vision, the people perish." Here Prashanth Shanmugan, a geopolitical strategist, writer, and humanitarian, goes on to say:

"When there is no passion it is the leaders who perish."

He believes that the art of leadership rests on three pillars: Passion, Vision, and Mission. He also wrote an article on the same.

Anyone from any organization, institution, or corporation, whether private or public, will proudly and boldly talk about their vision and mission statements. However, when asked about their passion, they fail to give any indication as to what it is.

Many leadership experts and books on management focus on the need for vision but overlook the importance of passion. Passion is the "Fire in the Belly", the driving force. It is the thing that propels people into action. People with a high intensity of fire in their bellies do not need an alarm to wake up each morning and start the new day. Their passion propels them. Passionate people are optimistic, have a great story, involve people, and have a simple, recharge strategy.

Simply put, Passion is what makes you live; not just exist. Vision is your long-term goal. In other words, it is what you want to do with your life. Mission is how you will go about it; and what action you will take to reach your goal.

What one should work on and think about is a "Passion Statement". What we need to do to be great leaders is to harness and instil passion, attain a common vision, and make the mission fulfilling for all.

The fire in the belly is indispensable. It is the inner drive that keeps you passionately moving forward even in the face of opposition and obstacles. Leaders must be intrinsically motivated by a deep determination to NOT GIVE UP. They must possess a strong passion, purpose, conviction, and commitment to keep taking courage and taking initiative for the greater good. That's the fire in the belly.

Patty Vogan, CEO of TEC International, shares a valuable tip on how to become a successful leader. She believes that as a leader, you must have passion. Your employees want passion. In fact, they'll go to the ends of the earth because of it, live and die for it. Think of the sailors who travelled with Christopher Columbus to explore uncharted territory. Their leader's passion inspired them to take on new and very dangerous challenges. Passionate leaders spread passion to others through their love of life, doing new things, taking risks, being motivated, having a sense of urgency, and reinventing themselves.

To build an extraordinary management team, you've got to light the "fire in their bellies" to get them to feel passionate about the company, institute, or organization and connect to the leader's vision. Passion is such a key part of being a great leader that if you don't have it, you can't impart it and you simply can't be a great leader. All the great leaders throughout the ages: Names like Nelson Mandela, Gandhi, Hitler, Alexander the Great, Genghis Khan, Leonardo da Vinci, Pablo Picasso, and Abraham Lincoln had passion.

This passion is infectious: when you talk about your vision for the country, company, or even a purpose. Others feel it and want to get on board. It is important to have passion for your vision.

Passion, purpose, commitment, and hard work are part of the fire in the belly. The question is: Can one impart, train, teach, or equip people with passion? When recruiting new team members, it is important to share the vision and mission of the organization and, more importantly, clearly and honestly talk about the challenges that would need to be overcome as a team and the effort/hard work it would entail. Find out if the prospective incumbent buys into this given their situation in life. viz. personal life issues such as health, family, and other interests,  impede working long hours or travel out of town. Many people when looking for a job that seems well-paying or prestigious, say yes to anything. Get behind it to the truth of the person. Profile tool testing could be used as a supplement to personal interaction.

Later the test also needs to be part of the performance review to check if it is still burning. What is also important is that it needs to be part of your expectations of yourself.

A key quality every leader needs to have is passion. However, that passion isn't an outspoken or dramatic quality. True passion requires honestly committing to something about which you feel deeply and staying committed through difficult circumstances. The following are indicators that a leader has true passion:
1. Passionate leaders genuinely believe in what they espouse. They engage people by the genuineness of their passion
2. They convey the power of their belief without dismissing or belittling others' points of view
3. Their passion is balanced with openness to others' points of view
4. Their actions support their beliefs
5. They stay committed despite the numerous challenges they face

When a leader is passionate, people feel a deep sense of being led in a worthy direction by someone who is committed to something more important than his or her own individual glory. Passion inspires. With passionate leaders, people feel included in the leader's commitment, as they feel they play a part in making important things happen. That is satisfying on a very deep level.

In the words of Simon Sinek, *"People don't buy what you do; they buy why you do it."* Leaders who know why they do what they do, who share their purpose with their team, and who make people believe in the pain-point the business is addressing, will inspire people. If everyone is behind the purpose and genuinely wants to play a role in solving customer problems, and they feel comfortable putting their hand up and saying, "Here's what we could do to achieve that", it can be transformative.

So, what's your purpose? Identify it and share it. Tell people why you do what you do, how that aligns with the goals and values of the business, and what role they can play in achieving those goals.

Leadership is Building Relationships

Human beings are naturally social animals who need positive interaction whether at work or with family and friends.

In terms of work-based relationships – the better our relationships are at work, the happier and more productive we are. Work becomes more enjoyable, and people are more willing to go along with changes that are to be implemented. We are more innovative and creative.

The key is to create a good working relationship with internal team members as well as external stakeholders, customers, investors, and government agencies. This will benefit everyone involved and the organization at large.

Some behaviours that help create a good, healthy working environment:
1. Trust: Every good relationship is based on trust. Building trust between you and your team, colleagues, customers, and stakeholders makes work and communication more effective and productive.
2. Mutual respect: It is a two-way street. You respect the people you work with, and they will respect you. Accept their ideas and inputs and they will value yours. Work together to solve problems and overcome obstacles collectively. This will eventually benefit everyone and the organization as a whole.
3. Open communication: We communicate all day whether through electronic media or face-to-face. The more open, honest, and effective you are in communicating with others, the better your relationships will be.

4. Mindfulness: This means taking responsibility for your actions and words. People who are mindful of

LEADERSHIP: THE PAST, THE PRESENT, & THE FUTURE

what they do, and what and how they speak to others don't let their own negative emotions impact people around them.

5. Welcoming diversity: Don't just accept diverse people and opinions but welcome them. Be open-minded and not just listen to what others at work have to say, whoever they may be. Consider their views while making decisions.
6. Be goal-directed: Make specific goals with timelines so time management is crucial for a successful leader, whether done with team members, support, or technology.
7. Be Positive: Being positive creates a feel-good environment all around.
8. Listen Actively: Practice listening actively more than just talking while interacting with anyone. People like to know that they are being heard and understood. Remove any distractions and pay attention to what the person is saying.
9. Appreciate Others: Whether the job is big or small, boss or doorman, thank them when they help you with anything. Complementing the work done by others helps build good relationships and solicits commitment. Humans crave appreciation.

One needs to be conscious of the need to spend time on relationship building and spend time on it. A broad-based approach to connecting with clients, teams, colleagues, friends, and family yields not just good business results but also personal happiness. Keep track of birthdays and special occasions. With technology, it is very easy to do so in a virtual systems calendar and the use of online technologies available.

In his book *Leadership and the Culture of Trust,* Gilbert W. Fairholm wrote:

"*In reality, leadership is an expression of collective community action. Leadership is something that happens as a result of leader and stakeholder collaborative action. Leadership is not a starring role. True leadership describes unified action of leaders and followers (stakeholders) working together to jointly achieve mutual goals. It is collaborative.*"

Collaboration is what is required in any organization. How the leader motivates and drives people to work together is what the outcome depends on.

Leaders believe in their values, vision, and goals for an organization or a cause and communicate them with others. Communication is a very important tool in building relationships and motivating people. They develop a feeling of commitment towards a common goal along with a common set of values.

To quote the business philosopher Peter F. Drucker:
"Every enterprise requires commitment to common goals and shared values."

In *The Leadership Challenge,* James M. Kouzes and Barry Z. Posner say:
"When leadership is a relationship founded on trust and confidence, people take risks, make changes, keep organizations and movements alive. Through that relationship, leaders turn their constituents into leaders themselves."

When you have a meaningful relationship with another person, you work more effectively together. You have a common goal and a consistent purpose. Your efforts are channelled toward the same common outcome.

Leaders interact with a diverse group of people right from their bosses, colleagues, juniors, customers, stakeholders, government agents, etc. They need to constantly change without losing their basic value, characteristics, and vision.

While working with their teams, they need to communicate their goals, motivate them, coach them, and foster trust and collaboration. They need to sometimes firefight and teach them how to work together. Let them think for themselves and listen to their ideas.

While dealing with customers, they need to instil trust. Listen to their grievances if any, and treat them like human beings, and not just to get money out of them.

Shareholders need to be researched and understood, and their requirements need to be addressed. They need to trust you, so regular, honest, and transparent communication is a must.

Leaders need to be open and honest in their communication, as this will help build trust, commitment, and continued long-term relationships that will benefit all.

People are at the centre of all leadership efforts. Leaders cannot lead unless they understand the people they are leading. One way to look at leadership is that the function of a leader is to lead and guide people who will follow the same values. An effective leader thus must be able to build relationships and create communities. We can define leadership as *"inspiring people and planning for the future with the motivating factors of relationship-building and community service"*. Relationships can happen among concepts, actions, and values. As for communities, one of the great advantages especially in higher education circles is leveraging the communities that exist for many different disciplines, interests, and practices. These communities provide, for anyone who wants to participate, opportunities to network and become involved with others who share similar values.

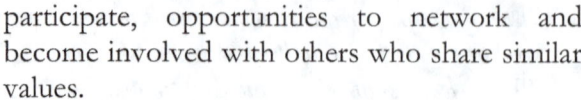

Values are important ideals that guide our priorities and are core to an organization. Values tie people together, set vision, and affect what we do as organizations and communities.

Leaders today need essential characteristics to build, guide, and maintain their organizations and communities. Some of these qualities include thinking for the future and developing a vision. It is important to set goals and to realize that change can happen along the way. Leaders must recognize their own initiative, want to lead, and be willing to assume responsibility. Motivation can take on many meanings — from creating the incentive for good project outcomes to guiding a vision that gives your followers energy and direction.

Commitment to the cause for the values of the group is also necessary for a good leader. Through commitment, we find more meaning in our work and service, and when we find more meaning in our work and service, we find value. As John W. Gardner said in his book *On Leadership*:

"Leaders must not only have their own commitments, they must move the rest of the team toward commitment."

It is easy to lead for yourself. It is more difficult to lead for others. Honesty, integrity, and the ability to be supportive will create a more successful environment. We all want to know that our leaders are deserving of our trust. It's about having trust in their knowledge of who and what they are  leading, trust in why they have chosen to lead and trust in their ability to accomplish the vision and goals that have been set forward.

Another way leaders can grow themselves and the people around them is to identify where relationship-building can be maintained and where it can be strengthened. Connecting with others is one of the most effective ways one can lead. In *The Leadership Challenge,* James M. Kouzes and Barry Z. Posner say:

"When leadership is a relationship founded on trust and confidence, people take risks, make changes, and keep organizations and movements alive. Through that relationship, leaders turn their constituents into leaders themselves."

In both maintaining and strengthening relationships, it is important to value people for who they are. Ask questions, really listen, and develop a mutual commitment. Encouraging others to take a chance, going along with them even when you don't know what the outcomes will be, and having the courage to support their decisions is something you can do to help lead. You must also develop your own communication skills and in turn, help others to develop theirs. Communication is a very powerful strategy when you are working to accomplish a goal. Making sure that you and your expectations are understood will benefit everyone. This will help you focus on teamwork and the prioritization of goals—which is especially important since it takes a group to attain those goals.

Relationship leaders have distinct methods that differ from title-driven or command-and-control leaders. Yet they still have a strong focus on results.

Becoming a Relationship-Focused Leader

A relationship leader is direct, truthful, and open. People want to work with leaders who can make decisions. However, being decisive also means building consensus when appropriate. Relationship leaders have versatile approaches and understand when to slow down and solicit ideas or ask questions. The ability to probe effectively leaves your team feeling like you're curious about their perspective.

Relationship leaders also shy away from edicts and command-like methods. Today's workforce doesn't respond to a "because I'm the boss" rationale.

Before they can trust others, leaders need to trust themselves, trust in their own decisions, and trust in the direction the company is going. If you know your purpose, this becomes quite simple. Decisions are made by asking: does this action align with my purpose?

When people work together, they can build the impossible. This is what we need to do as leaders. This is the revolution that we need to kickstart. If we have a purpose, if we trust, and if we give people a voice and actually listen to them, we can build ourselves up and build up the people around us. In doing so, we can build our business to grow in a scalable, sustainable, and people-led way.

How can you get people to trust in your decisions as a leader? Finally, and most importantly, how can you make them part of those decisions?

One has heard of crocodile tears, i.e., faking sorry. However, there can also be crocodile smiles. Children being innocent and perceptive can pick up when a parent is pretending to smile even when angry. They know a crocodile smile from a genuine one. Humans are all actually perceptive of this but over time some of us get de-sensitive. In an organization, leaders who are open and honest and do not hesitate to even acknowledge their own weaknesses and mistakes evoke much greater respect and commitment from their teams. Putting on a brave front, hiding their mistakes, or exhibiting crocodile smiles don't work.

Empathy is not sympathy. It is understanding peoples' situations and extending help if needed and as feasible. When one cares for people when they have emotional issues, it builds a better bond, both professional and personal.

Giving credit and recognition freely and openly helps fuel creativity.

Humility is a virtue that pays rich dividends. However, there are leaders who have been arrogant and yet succeeded.

Teamwork is Key

As leaders look beyond the top ranks for creative direction, they must combat what is known as the lone inventor myth. Though past breakthroughs have sometimes come from a single genius, the reality today is that most innovations draw on many contributions. Even in today's highly networked world, organizations fail to take full advantage of internet technologies to tap into the creativity of many smart people working on the same problem.

Robert Sutton, a professor at Stanford University's School of Engineering, noted that most companies have hierarchical structures, and this hierarchy impedes the exchange of ideas between levels.

Be Open to Diverse Perspectives

Innovation is more likely when people of different disciplines, backgrounds, and areas of expertise share their thinking. Sometimes, the complexity of a problem demands diversity. Managers can also enhance diversity by looking outside the organization for sources of creativity.

Empowerment and Trust

Empowerment and trust go hand in hand. If you want to empower someone to do a certain job or carry out a certain role, you have to trust their judgement and ideas. Give them the freedom to carry out their duties and complete the task their way. It can be frustrating and scary to have someone watch them like a hawk. This lowers their confidence and affects their work.

If leaders want their employees to trust them, they must trust them in return. Trust begets trust. It is up to the leader to take the initiative and begin to trust their team first, before expecting their trust. For any business to grow, trust is a must. If there is a lack of trust between the leaders and their teams, the atmosphere in the workplace is fuelled with negative energy due to which there is an overall feeling of apathy which in turn leads to low productivity, attrition, and the eventual downfall of the organization.

People do not only work for their salaries at the end of the month; they also look for job satisfaction. They need to feel needed. They need to know that their work counts for something; this gives them a sense of responsibility for their work.

Steve Jobs famously said:

"It doesn't make sense to hire smart people and tell them what to do; we hire smart people so they can tell us what to do."

Leaders need to show their employees that they trust them. When they give them an assignment, they cannot sit on their heads telling them what to do and how exactly to do it all the time. Once the initial handholding is done, let go of the reigns. Let the employees use their own ideas and be innovative and creative in their work. The leaders should be open to listening and accepting them in order to build confidence and trust.

Openness to new ideas can lead to improved productivity and greater

revenue. Organizations need to constantly modify their structures and policies to keep up with the changing times. Organizations that value their employees' ideas and act on them are more likely to grow whereas those that do not, tend to stagnate.

In order to build trust, managers also need to communicate honestly and openly with their teams, explaining how processes work and the reason behind the decisions that are taken. Employees who feel trusted and cared about will, in turn, trust and work more diligently for the manager and company, thereby increasing productivity.

Managers need to empower their employees by delegating duties and work. Managers should not feel insecure about their position, or they will hesitate to delegate any work to their subordinates.

Managers need to understand that no successful business or company is a one-man show. It is a collective effort of several people. They need to encourage their employees to take more responsibility by giving them reasonable authority and freedom to work. This makes them feel more empowered, satisfied, trusted, and responsible, and they tend to take ownership of their actions. It makes them want to contribute more. Empowerment and trust create a healthy, positive, and ultimately successful company that benefits everyone.

It can be difficult to break out of the leader-follower mindset in the workplace. In fact, researchers from Penn State, Claremont McKenna College, and Tsinghua University found that only rare "transformational leaders" are able to prevent employees from being excessively reliant on their bosses, cultivating instead a staff that feels empowered and self-guided. Trust and business acumen are some of the cornerstones in building this type of work culture. This wisdom can be used to train informed and decisive teams.

Some possible ways to empower employees and get back precious time:
1. Encourage a Culture of Feedback: Instant, on-the-spot feedback is one way for your team to communicate workflow issues to one another so that proper action can be taken right away. Make sure to set ground rules for this feedback – it must be both constructive and respectful. Essentially, you want your team to trust you and each

other to deliver honest and helpful praise and criticism.

2. Share Information: Host regular meetings with your team and share with them the large happenings within your organization. Help your team understand the main goals that you're driving towards. Give them a rundown on how other divisions are performing – the more pieces of the puzzle your team gains, the more 'buy-in' and cooperation it will beget.

3. Present New Challenges and Opportunities: It is important to challenge your employees so they can demonstrate and achieve their full potential. For example, you might notice that your sales representative tends to rely heavily on email interactions – challenge them to get on the phone instead and get outside of their comfort zone. You can also work with their unique interests and abilities – for example, you might notice

that an employee loves to assist their team with processes. Invite this person to lead a customer workshop, so that they can develop their presentation skills and build stronger client bonds. Or you might discover that a co-worker is bilingual and ask him to work with international customers. If you're out of ideas, sit down with each member of your team and ask them what types of experiences would help them grow professionally.

4. Give Flexibility: Examine your workflow and identify key areas that would benefit from greater flexibility and creative input. These tasks might include content creation, marketing strategies, and company events. Sit down with your team and explain how much flexibility they will each have within a task. Don't leave it open-ended – give them some parameters to work with so that they're not overwhelmed with options.

5. Delegate Authority with Responsibility: Give your team some space, trust them, and you might be impressed by what they're able to achieve. The quality of a leader can be judged by the standards and goals they set for themselves and not being afraid to fail. As an old saying goes, *"Aim for the sun and even if you reach the moon, you have done*

a great job." Breaking out of the traditional leader-follower mindset can help you create stronger staff bonds founded on trust, self-confidence, and achievement. When you create room for independent work and decision-making, your team might discover that they're able to achieve far more than they originally thought possible.

9 LEADERSHIP QUALITIES NEEDED TO SUCCEED

Being a learner is a big leadership challenge.

The leaders at the top need to be constantly informed on development, not just locally but globally, because the technology of the internet and the telecom revolution has made the world a global village. So, knowledge is power and knowledge ahead of others can give a winning edge.

Leaders need to build relationships, more so than ever before, with all stakeholders like suppliers, vendors, clients, customers, governments/regulators, and above all, employees. This will enable them to be well-informed of developments in their immediate environment and way beyond. They must establish trust with all these groups of people.

In the age of high attrition, hiring and retention of good talent is an increasing challenge. Communication and engagement with employees are crucial. Ensuring training, recognition, and rewarding is increasingly important. Often, the best talent is lured away.

Being regularly informed about directly and indirectly relevant technology is becoming increasingly important, with the rapid development of technologies in all areas.

Dr. Mahathir Mohamad became the Prime Minister of Malaysia for the second time at the age of 94. He regretted that in his first tenure, after the first few years of focusing on Malaysia's development, he got caught

up in political manoeuvrings. The same seemed to have happened in his second tenure. However, in a speech at the Setia City Convention Centre, he mentioned the following qualities needed to be a successful and good leader:
1. Integrity
2. Hard work
3. Constantly updating knowledge and awareness of change
4. Humility
5. Walking the talk and leading from the front

Leadership lesson from Salvador Dali:

Salvador Dali was an eccentric artist who lived, dressed, and painted in a very different style, giving rise to the surrealist style of art. His thinking and behaviour verged on madness. Yet he pulled it off and became a legend as did his paintings which got acclaimed as unique works of art.

Psychologists call the same way of thinking all the time, which most of us do, as Personal Construct Theory, while Dali-thinking is described as Propositional Theory, where any way of thinking, even radically different, can yield amazing outcomes, as did Dali's paintings. When leaders explore unknown territories, new and different possibilities arise.

Leaders Need to Constantly Learn

"There is something to be learned every day both by looking in the mirror at yourself and by looking at people around you."
~Antoni Cimolino (Artistic Director of the Stanford Shakespeare)

Learning, like change, never stops. It is a constant process. Every day you learn something new, either from your own experiences and mistakes, from your environment, or from those around you.

Just like how young children are sponges – they absorb everything they see and hear from their environment – successful leaders must constantly absorb everything and implement new ideas appropriately.

Leaders in successful companies often like to recruit people who are smarter than themselves so that they can learn from them, which in turn keeps the company competitive and ensures continued success.

Leaders must be wary of falling into the trap of thinking that they are the boss and therefore know everything. The *"it's my way or the highway"* attitude will get them and the organization nowhere. It is detrimental to all and alienates them from everyone.

Leaders need to keep abreast of what is happening in the world as well as in their immediate surroundings. They must be open to learning and changing as rapidly if not faster than these changes.

Learning can happen from various sources, from just talking to people or from media in all its forms. Being open to learning at all times will not only benefit the leaders personally but also professionally, thus improving the performance of the organizations they manage.

Another way an individual or organization can improve productivity is by encouraging training, whether it is a one-to-one training or a group. Sharing and learning from one another's experiences also goes a long way and benefits both individuals and the organization as a whole. Progressive organizations understand the importance of developing their people through regular and meaningful training, thus investing in their future success.

Thinking Outside the Box

Though much clichéd, thinking out of the box has a lot of relevance.

At a basic level, it is about being aware of new technologies, competitors, activities, customer tastes, national and global regulations and agreements, and the values and ways of life of the new generations.

For example, technological developments have dramatically impacted the publishing business and bookstores with online publishing. Those that either got on to the trip of doing likewise or diversified into related products have survived and thrived; those that did not have had to shut down.

If competitors have emerged with offering new products or ways of doing business, one needs to watch out.

Starbucks has offered a new lifestyle as opposed to stopping for a cup of coffee, with food, Wi-Fi, and a casual free-from-purchase pressure to work out of their stores.

With the boom of social media, new styles in the fashion of clothing, shoes, and accessories from Milan, Paris, or New York get known, and demand is created overnight as soon as visuals are shared on social media. So, fashion houses in Mumbai or Nairobi had better adapt fast or pack up.

Everyone is now in appreciation of Uber, Airbnb, airline ticket booking portals, etc. that have leveraged internet tech developments.

Such disruptive businesses are the outcomes of such different thinking. Likewise, with foodstuffs, fast foods are getting rapidly localised to meet local tastes. The young in India and China want burgers and fried chicken but with a spicy, sweet, or localised version.

Besides learning quickly from the environment, one needs to see if one can be proactive and predict change, or even create change. Identify latent demand for products. There is a famous story of two salespersons who were sent to explore the market for shoes in a remote African village decades ago way before the advent of the internet social media and cell phones. One came back and said there was no demand for shoes since no one wears shoes. The other said there is a huge demand for shoes since no one makes or sells shoes here, so no one wears them. So, moving from demand-led supply to creating demand by providing supplies, is the lesson learned.

The World Trade Agreements, though still being battled over for national interest by countries and groups of countries, have yet nonetheless come to many breakthrough agreements on tariffs, import duties, and taxes, enabling proactive companies to move in quickly to export or set up manufacturing facilities.

Creative and innovative ideas for product enhancement to even existing products can yield and have yielded first mover advantage to some companies. While faster cell phone speeds are what companies are battling to be first in the market, some have realized that the camera function and its enhancement of the quality of pictures and sharing them is a major factor considered in the buying decision by some people, especially youngsters who are constantly sharing photos real-time of their ongoing lives. This sharing of pictures of oneself has created a boom in beauty products, salons, and beauty parlour businesses. As economies grow and people in developing nations move up the financial and social ladder and have more disposable income, higher-end clothing and fashion businesses have grown.

Catching trends in time is key, but inventing the future is the real entrepreneurial and technological challenge.

Jack Welch, the man who made General Electric into a huge conglomerate says that leaders must have the courage to make unpopular decisions and gut calls.

What are gut calls? Gut calls are intuition. What is intuition? It is not some magical spiritual quality that comes from heaven. It is, in fact, the distilled information, knowledge, and wisdom that a leader has acquired from his childhood years to the current moment of being nurtured, now coming together as instinct or as an idea.

Why do people not leave the box? Because it is safer in the box. Getting out of the box is to risk change. Most people abhor change. Also, leaving the box is risky and can be expensive. It is not easy to put your neck on the line. As a leader within an organization, you risk expensive mistakes and of course, the ability to get the approval of your boss who may be more cautious.

At the top, making significant out-of-the-box changes like entering unchartered territories or investing in new technologies may bomb, and this may invoke shareholder wrath and a share price tumble risk. But, *"no risk, no gain"*. Fortune favours the brave.

Mark Zuckerberg was ridiculed when he started working on Facebook, as were the Wright brothers who put the first plane in flight.

Bill Gates initially rejected the idea of a computer having more than 640k memory.

Fred Smith's idea to create an overnight delivery service got him a

C grading for that idea from his professor at Yale University for being impractical. He went on to form Federal Express.

The Beatles were rejected by the Decca Recording Co. as they thought that guitar music was outdated.

The radio was rejected for investment by David Sarnoff Co. as a useless box.

The Warner Brothers rejected the idea of actors talking in movies.

People who questioned conventional wisdom in the Middle Ages were not just ridiculous but imprisoned and put to death. Hence, creative people who think outside the box not only need to come up with crazy ideas but also be brave to withstand the consequences. They need to be persistent.

Good leaders need to not only think outside the box but encourage their teams to do it. They can't come up with all the ideas themselves. They must listen, no matter how outlandish the idea sounds. Brainstorming sessions are a way to encourage out-of-the-box thinking, then allotting resources to the best ones and pursuing them. For thinking outside the box, look not just for logical or data-based reasons for ideas but also for hunches and intuition. Invite customers, suppliers, and bankers besides the internal team to brainstorm ideas. They know your product or service from a different angle. Get outsiders from other businesses to give inputs. Create informal advisory boards and professional associations. Build social and other interests to broaden your outlook to get ideas that are different.

Overcoming Roadblocks in Innovation

Why is it so challenging for companies to innovate? There are many reasons of course, and it is hard to distil them down to just one simple reason. One challenge is that people are fundamentally very resistant to change. When you're in a bad situation, you're eager to change, and that's a positive thing. But often, when people are in a good or even just a bearable situation, they are very resistant to change (sometimes without really being aware of this fact). We all intuitively know that people don't generally like change in these contexts. The scientific question is why we are so resistant to change. One answer can be found in behavioural economics, in the psychology of decision-making. Daniel Kahneman, the Nobel laureate, found that when you give somebody a quantity of something – money, a trip, food, a bonus at work – they experience some amount of subjective pleasure. If you take the same thing away from the person once they already have it, it gives them much more pain than they experienced in getting it in the first place. Put more simply, negative things have about two to three times the impact on us psychologically as positive things do.

Another important point is that whether we experience something as positive or negative depends very much on a person's frame of reference. For example, if you give an employee a €10,000 bonus, they could interpret that as a wonderful thing and be very happy. But if they find out that a colleague got a €15,000 bonus, now all of a sudden this bonus is no longer €10,000; it's negative €5000. So, they're on the other negative side of the curve, even though they've received a large sum of money. Hence, in the world of gains and losses, what people experience psychologically is very subjective.

Taken together, these findings shed light on why people resist change. Because negative things have roughly two to three times the impact on us as positive things. For people to be willing to make a change, the positives of the proposed change have to outweigh the negatives by a factor of about two or three. Unfortunately, that's not always easy to do when you're proposing a change, because people are already doing something a certain way, and they often frame situations mentally more in terms of the tangible costs of what they give up, and less in terms of the often fewer tangible benefits that might be gained.

This is often particularly true with changes involving investment or projects. When you make a change, you pay for it now, but the benefits usually come later. So, there's a delay in the positives, while the negative of investing the money happens now. Many things work against us, and what we find is that innovation is often hard because people don't like to change. The benefits of the innovation need to far outweigh the negatives, that is, the cost of the innovation, not objectively, but psychologically. Often, the people who propose innovations at companies spend a lot of time building a business case – an argument – for why the innovation needs to happen, and why the planned change is better than the current way of doing things. What they don't focus on enough is the psychological case for why the change needs to happen. They don't sufficiently take into consideration the psychological negatives of what people are going to perceive when they lose. And they don't sufficiently take into account the psychological positives that they could put into place to make the change more compelling.

That's a very important reason why innovation is difficult – because you have to overcome this psychological change barrier that we know about from compelling behavioural research.

10 FEEDBACK

Feedback at work or even in personal life is a sensitive issue. It is not just about what is said in feedback; but when it is given and how it is given.

The objective is to get a better understanding of strengths and weaknesses, and the skills that need upgrading via training, on-the-job learning, attitude, communication, or behaviour. In fact, feedback is needed for almost any aspect of human activity and behaviour that impacts productivity and relationships at work and in families.

Companies have a system of feedback as part of the HR learning and development function. It is usually a part of an annual 360-degree review process. It can be given via a written procedure by juniors, peers, and supervisors, or can be given personally in private. The objective is to improve efficiency and focus at work. Often, individuals welcome honest feedback from someone they respect and trust. Depending on what the issue or the personality of the individual is, feedback is a sensitive area of organizational functioning.

While the objective of providing feedback is to give objective inputs and help the person find ways to improve, if not handled well it can demoralize and cause loss of interest in work and reduce productivity. At a personal level, it can improve or mar relationships.

Anonymous feedback encourages more frankness and eliminates fear about the relationship getting affected. However, the receiver of the feedback may feel low and confused and wonder who provided the feedback. If the anonymous feedback was negative, it may result in second-guessing, reducing focus on work, causing stress, and marring good relationships.

Feedback should be open, honest, and with a goal to help the person do better. When done in this manner, it can instil behavioural changes that enable people to become more effective, more efficient, and more fulfilled at work.

Most people feel that they would do better if they received corrective feedback in a positive manner from the right person to enable them to improve; for instance, their managers.

Good relationships with family members, friends, and colleagues are associated with several important emotional and health outcomes, including a lower risk of depression and enhanced job satisfaction and engagement. In the sports arena, feedback is given through encouragement and motivational pep talk by coaches. Peers also give feedback to each other on the sports team as the objective is clearly to win as a team, as this is the only way in team sports.

Neurological science has given useful insights into feedback-giving. The prospect of receiving feedback is often viewed as possible criticism and hence raises stress levels and results in the fight or flight response in the brain.

Ken Blanchard said, *"Feedback is the breakfast of champions"*. In the same way that a good breakfast supplies us with the energy we need to get through the day, feedback is the fuel an organization needs to perform at its best.

It is not just positive feedback that people crave either. According to research by Harvard Business Review (HBR), 72% of people feel their performance would improve if their managers provided corrective feedback, i.e., suggestions for improvement. In fact, 57% said they would prefer corrective feedback to positive praise or recognition. We all want to be the best we can be, and constructive feedback gives us the opportunity to learn and grow.

Feedback is an important factor in defining the quality of our relationships, both at home and at work. Strong relationships with your partner, family members, friends, and colleagues are significantly associated with several important emotional and health outcomes, including a lower risk of burnout and depression as well as enhanced job satisfaction and engagement.

However, research into the neurobiology of feedback has given us some important clues about why feedback can sometimes do more harm than good.

Social evaluation and rejection tend to activate the same neural pathways associated with physical pain. So, when we experience being evaluated, criticised, or judged, it triggers a stress reaction. It activates the part of the brain that launches the fight or flight response.

This is something we can all relate to. Just hearing the words, *"Can I give you some feedback?"*, can put us on edge. We have come to assume that feedback means bad news.

In a professional setting, most of us are not taught to recognise what is going well. Instead, we are taught to identify what is going wrong and to fix it. It is therefore natural that feedback can make us a bit defensive, as we want to know that we are valued and recognised and that people see us in a positive light.

The knock-on effect is that if people feel hurt or rejected by the negative feedback they receive at work, they may become less satisfied and engaged. And their performance will suffer as a result.

One of the most widely cited studies on performance feedback found that in a third of all studies on feedback interventions, individual performance declined, rather than improved. Although they speculated about many reasons why feedback led to worse performance, they suggested that in most cases it is because it had led to individuals feeling hurt, demotivated, and emotionally upset.

Researchers revealed there may be a tipping point for discomfort in how much negative versus positive feedback we receive. Those who received a small number of unfavourable behaviourally-based comments improved more than other managers. Those who received a large number (relative to positive comments) significantly declined in performance more than their peers. They concluded that if the ratio of positive to negative feedback is low, individuals can become disengaged and demoralised.

Anonymous versus Non-Anonymous Feedback Methods

Organizations have traditionally used 360-degree feedback tools, where feedback is given anonymously. This is usually a part of an annual review process. However, this anonymous and structured approach to giving feedback is at odds with the open, feedback-rich culture that the modern workforce increasingly demands.

The Pros and Cons of Anonymous Feedback

The biggest benefit of feedback being given anonymously is that people tend to feel more comfortable sharing their opinions and observations. People can be especially uncomfortable giving feedback to those in more senior roles for fear that they will be punished in some way, or because they don't want to seem to be treading on toes. By keeping it anonymous, people are often open and honest in their evaluations.

Recipients may also find comfort in not knowing who said what about them. If they knew someone had made a negative comment about them it may change how they act towards them, for example. By not knowing, they can take it on board and quietly adapt their future behaviour.

There are, however, many reasons why an anonymous approach to feedback may not be the best method. The reality is that while anonymity can help bring an issue to a person's awareness, it does not necessarily help them to solve it.

Individuals can often feel offended, hurt, or simply bewildered by the information they receive. The anonymous approach can also lead to hours of distraction as recipients try to decipher which comment was made by whom. More importantly, there is no opportunity to ask the person who gave the feedback why they scored them a certain way or said what they did so that they can better understand it, accept it, and move forward.

Anonymity simply makes it difficult for the individual to act on the feedback they have been given. The knock-on effect is that they may actually end up feeling disheartened, unmotivated, and even resentful of their colleagues. Equally, they may simply forget about it, leaving the report in a drawer and not acting on the feedback they've been given.

The Benefits of an Open Feedback Approach

By taking away anonymity, feedback becomes richer, more valuable, and meaningful. It encourages people to take ownership of the feedback they give, resulting in more carefully considered responses. It minimises the risk of vague or petty comments being made. People are more direct and more focused. This greater openness and clarity results in far more actionable feedback. You find people saying, *"I didn't know that person thought that about me. I need to go and have a conversation with them."*

An open feedback approach is not just about peer-to-peer feedback. It can help to create a more open, honest, and collaborative environment where everyone feels valued.

Challenges of Creating an Open Feedback Culture

Before we take a look at how to create an open feedback culture, let's take a moment to address the challenges.

Firstly, although people are ready to hear constructive feedback, they are not always ready or indeed know how to give it. A study by Harvard Business Review revealed that people tend to avoid giving negative feedback and are much more comfortable giving positive feedback.

This is not completely surprising. Giving negative or constructive feedback can be awkward and uncomfortable. We don't know how the individual will react; if they will be hurt or upset, become defensive, or even take us seriously. And what happens if we say something that doesn't fit with the ideology of the organization? How will we then be perceived? People can find it particularly challenging to give feedback to their managers and other more senior people, even in an anonymous setting.

Secondly, if people are only used to giving feedback formally, at annual reviews and appraisals, how do we shift to a culture where people feel comfortable giving feedback readily, and positively make the effort to do so on a daily basis?

Finally, how do we change people's attitudes toward feedback? We tend to associate feedback with things that have gone wrong, but feedback can be positive too. Changing people's mindsets to use feedback for praise and recognition as well is a vital step in encouraging an open culture.

Using the Management by Objectives Approach

Management By Objectives (MBO) is a performance management approach developed by Peter Drucker, in which a balance is sought between the objectives of employees and the company goals, to determine joint objectives and provide feedback on the results. Setting challenging but attainable objectives promotes motivation and empowerment of employees and creates a performance-based work environment. By increasing commitment, managers are given the opportunity to focus on new ideas and innovations that contribute to the development and objectives of organizations.

Since this method of performance management has been designed to improve performance at all levels within an organization, a comprehensive evaluation system is therefore essential. As goals and objectives have been SMART formulated, they make the evaluation of processes very easy. Employees are evaluated and rewarded for their achievements in relation to the set goals and objectives. This also includes accurate feedback. Management By Objectives is about why, when, and how objectives can be achieved.

11 QUOTES AND LESSONS FROM LEGENDS

Leadership at one time, I suppose, meant muscles. Today it means getting along with people.
— Mahatma Gandhi

The growth and development of people is the highest calling of leadership.
— Harvey Firestone

Treat people as if they were what they ought to be and you help them to become what they are capable of being.
— Johann Goethe

Leadership is the capacity to translate vision into reality.
— Warren Bennis

Leadership is the art of getting someone else to do something you want done, because they want to do it.
— Dwight Eisenhower

A leader is best when people barely know he exists. When his work is done, aim fulfilled, they will say: we did it ourselves.
— Lao Tzu

The art of leadership is learning to say no, not saying yes. It is easy to say yes.

LEADERSHIP: THE PAST, THE PRESENT, & THE FUTURE

— Tony Blair

Leaders aren't born, they are made. And they are made just like anything else, through hard work. And that's the price we'll have to pay to achieve that goal, or any goal.
— Vince Lombardi

The function of leadership is to produce more leaders, not more followers.
— Ralph Nader

The most important qualities of a good leader include integrity, accountability, empathy, humility, resilience, vision, influence and positivity.

Management is about persuading people to do things they do not want to do, while leadership is about inspiring people to do things, they never thought they could.

A man who dares to waste one hour of time has not discovered the value of life.
— Charles Darwin

Charles Darwin (1809 - 1882) was a naturalist and geologist who pioneered the field of evolutionary biology. If you want to accomplish as much as Darwin did in his lifetime, adhere to his advice and don't waste one single hour of your time.

You cannot teach a man anything; you can only help him discover it in himself.
— Galileo

Galileo Galilei (1564 – 1642) was an Italian astronomer, mathematician, physicist, and philosopher. Galileo's quote is one echoed for generations that one must learn something for themselves. Your mom may have told you the burner was hot as a kid, but you eventually tested it for yourself.

Shall I refuse my dinner because I do not fully understand the process of digestion?
— Oliver Heaviside

Oliver Heaviside (1850 – 1925) was an English mathematician and physicist working primarily in the electrical engineering field. The quote above is in reference to Heaviside using mathematical operators that were not yet clearly defined by the mathematics community.

If I have seen further, it is by standing on the shoulders of Giants.
– Isaac Newton

Sir Isaac Newton (1642 – 1727) wrote the quote above in his letter to rival Robert Hooke in 1676. Nothing is done in a vacuum; we must all stand on our forefathers to better ourselves and the world around us. Tackling the challenges of the world today will require that more than ever.

Two things are infinite: the universe and human stupidity; and I'm not sure about the universe.

– Albert Einstein

This quote, first appearing in Ego, Hunger, and Aggression: a Revision of Freud's Theory and Method by Frederick S. Perls. Einstein (1879 – 1955), is known to have clashed with popular thinking and the limited imagination of fellow scientists and the public.

Life cannot have had a random beginning...the trouble is that there are about 2000 enzymes, and the chance of obtaining them all in a random trial is only one part in $10^{40,000}$, an outrageously small probability that could not be faced even if the whole universe consisted of organic soup.
– Fred Hoyle

Sir Fred Hoyle (1915 – 2001), an astronomer, was known for controversial stances on scientific matters and contribution to stellar nucleosynthesis.

It is strange that only extraordinary men make the discoveries, which later appear so easy and simple.
– Georg C. Lichtenberg

Georg Lichtenberg (1742 – 1799) was a German experimental physicist known for satire. Science is built upon previous knowledge, which is incredible that what is now common-sense mathematics was once never before discovered or thought of.

There may be babblers, wholly ignorant of mathematics, who dare to condemn my hypothesis, upon the authority of some part of the Bible twisted to suit their purpose.

I value them not, and scorn their unfounded judgment.
– Nicolaus Copernicus

Nicolaus Copernicus (1473 – 1543) was a Polish Renaissance mathematician and astronomer known for proposing that the Sun, in fact, is the centre of the universe. Nicolaus' inspirational quote is ripe with anger and condemnation. This reminds us that religion and science have always lived parallelly, sometimes symbiotically, sometimes not.

There is no law except the law that there is no law.
– John Archibald Wheeler

John Archibald Wheeler (1911 – 2008) was an American theoretical physicist largely credited for reviving dialogue in general relativity. Here, John Wheeler reminds us that in nature and human imagination, anything is possible.

We pass through this world but once. Few tragedies can be more extensive than the stunting of life, few injustices deeper than the denial of an opportunity to strive or even to hope, by a limit imposed from without, but falsely identified as lying within.
– Stephen Jay Gould

Stephen Jay Gould (1941 – 2002) was an American palaeontologist and an expert in evolutionary biology. Dr. Gould developed the theory of punctuated equilibrium, whereby long periods of stability are punctuated by rare occurrences of branching evolution.

Falsity in intellectual action is intellectual immorality.
– Thomas Chrowder Chamberlin

Thomas Chamberlin's inspirational quote above was given during the 1888 University of Michigan Annual Commencement. Thomas Chamberlin (1843 – 1928) was an influential geologist who founded the Journal of Geology.

The black holes of nature are the most perfect macroscopic objects there are in the universe: the only elements in their construction are our concepts of space and time.
– Subrahmanyan Chandrasekhar

This quote from Subrahmanyan Chandrasekhar (1910 – 1995) appears in his book Mathematical Theory of Black Hole. Chandrasekhar was an Indian American astrophysicist and was awarded the Nobel Prize for Physics in 1983 for his mathematical theory on the structure and evolution of stars.

The saddest aspect of life right now is that science gathers knowledge faster than

society gathers wisdom.
— Isaac Asimov

Isaac Asimov (1920 – 1992) was an American biochemist and author. Asimov was a prolific science fiction and popular science writer.

The good thing about science is that it's true whether or not you believe in it.
— Neil deGrasse Tyson

Neil deGrasse Tyson's (1958 - present) quote from The Colbert Report distinguishes the difference between opinion and fact. Science, as a base, is always true, it is interpretation that imparts human error. Whether you believe in science or not is irrelevant.

Nothing in life is to be feared, it is only to be understood. Now is the time to understand more, so that we may fear less.
— Marie Curie

Marie Curie (1867 – 1934) was the first woman to be awarded a Nobel Prize in 1903 for her contributions to physics. She was again awarded the 1911 Nobel Prize for her contributions to chemistry. Although we may fear the unknown, it should not limit our desire to understand the unknown.

Equipped with his five senses, man explores the universe around him and calls the adventure Science.
— Edwin Powell Hubble

Edwin Hubble (1889 - 1953) was an American astronomer known for his significant contribution to astronomy including Hubble's Law. Hubble is known and regarded as one of the most influential observational cosmologists of the 20th century.

One, remember to look up at the stars and not down at your feet. Two, never give up work. Work gives you meaning and purpose and life is empty without it. Three, if you are lucky enough to find love, remember it is there and don't throw it away.
— Stephen Hawking

Great Leadership Speeches

Martin Luther King Jr.'s speech *I Have a Dream*, in front of an audience of 250,000 people in 1969 in the US to bring an end to racism and inequality, inspired millions of Americans—not only blacks, but all races, and drove a greater push for regulations to control racism and was driven more so after his assassination.

Steve Jobs' graduation speech at Stanford University in 2005 gives three lessons from his three stories:
1. Don't do what you don't like to do. Finding what you truly love and getting down to doing that increases the chances of success as you will work harder and give it your best.
2. If you fail or are fired, start over again and don't be destroyed. Again, do what you love and follow your dream.
3. Know that you will die, so fear not failure or what others think. Say or do and pursue what you like. Ask yourself if today is the last day of your life, would you still go out and do what you will do? If not, change tracks as soon as you can.

President Obama's speech at Cairo University in 2005 healed the tension brewing between the Islamic world and the West with a very honest and endearing speech.

12 LEADERSHIP IN POLITICS

Numerous researchers such as Weaver, Burns, Bath, Mirrel, and numerous others wrestled with the concept of leadership in politics. They have had divergent and complex understanding, that leadership is a process within a process.

Since politics is a process, and leadership within that a process, the objective is to understand political leadership which within social systems serves society.

The most common forms of political leadership which have developed in human societies since humans began to form social groups, have evolved into different forms as mentioned in the early part of this book.

Democracy, communism, and dictatorships have been the main broad forms of politics. These again have various forms such as presidential and parliamentary democracy with direct and indirect voting patterns. These have opposition parties and constitutions to ensure checks and balances. In dictatorships, at times, there is some semblance of democracy and voting processes but often found to be unfair or rigged. There have been democratically-elected political leaders who have gone on to function dictatorially, given that they assume the moral right by virtue of being elected and with little respect for opposition parties or views or debates.

There have also been good and bad dictatorial leaders.

Lee Kwan Liu of Singapore, Kamal Attaturk of Turkey, Mao Tse Tung of China, Stalin of Russia, and Fidel Castro of Cuba have been controversial. Nonetheless, they have transformed the shape of their nations and delivered high levels of social welfare, at times at the cost of the wealthier constituents of their nations.

The highest form of leadership is exercised at the highest levels of politics, since it controls authority for the enactment of the laws of the land, public policy, allocations of resources, geopolitical relationships, and security of the nation externally, to maintain the existential purpose of the nation and internal law, order and justice.

Good political leadership calls for high integrity, becoming increasingly rare in many nations these days. It calls for a conscience and consideration for the welfare of all people. It calls for open-mindedness to be receptive to all viewpoints be they relating to resource allocation, taxation, development prioritization, and diverse religious views and beliefs. It calls for the willingness to make decisions even at the risk of losing an election and needing to demit office and stand by principles of fairness and justice. It calls for the commitment to making decisions for the good of the vast majority of people in their constituency, be that national or regional. One must assume responsibility for the decisions that are made by the government and also assume accountability for wrong decisions.

Political leaders must have the resolve to resist pressures of vested interest groups, even with their own group and outsiders to make and pass laws favourable to them, and to not confer favors and appointments on the basis of pressures and financial incentives. One of the major sources of favouritism is often close family and friends.

One needs to be open to diverse opinions and ideas from different quarters including opposition parties. One needs to build consensus and make decisions even at the risk of becoming unpopular and losing an election. The danger is that power corrupts and absolute power corrupts absolutely.

Effective political leaders have leadership styles that focus on coalition and building, while ineffective political leaders are "hustlers" – i.e., those who use manipulation to get what they want, instead of inspiration and motivation. While negotiation and even coercion are sometimes necessary, a good political leader will always try to use persuasion first.

Unfortunately, there has been an increase in the criminalization of politics and criminals entering politics. In a democratic society, it is seemingly difficult to control this due to the belief and law of various forms of freedom. The legal system in a democracy gives an opportunity for criminals and other wrongdoers to escape punishment due to the slow legal process, giving the corrupt ample opportunity to escape punishment, get bail, and bribe witnesses, the police, and the judges. Politics is considered the best money-making business, on the shame of democracy.

Niccolò Machiavelli was an Italian philosopher who lived in Italy around 600 years ago and wrote several books, of which the most notable was *The Prince*. Machiavelli was influenced by philosophers Aristotle and Plato, and in turn influenced Rousseau and Hobbes. His name over the centuries has been perhaps unfairly associated with deception, manipulation, and deceit in political life.

Henry Kissinger who played a major role in diplomacy on behalf of the USA as Secretary of State during the Nixon presidency, has at times been considered Machiavellian in his global role to further US interest, especially in the Middle East.

He foresaw the growing importance of China when it was a minor power and got Nixon to travel to China for a 30-minute audience with Chairman Mao, while he conducted diplomacy with Chou En Lai, the Prime Minister of China, to build bridges with the communist regime, recognising it as a future global economic and military superpower.

Arvind Kejriwal from India, founder of the AAM ADMI PARTY – the Peoples' Party – focused on rooting out corruption and won a landslide victory in the state elections in India in 1993. He went on to walk the talk with an image of being a clean politician, a rare breed in India. However, in the National General Elections for Parliament, he was outclassed by the Narendra Modi wave that swept India. He still went on to provide free essential services such as electricity, water, and subsidised transport to again sweep the elections in the next State Elections in 2020. So, a leader in a poor country who can provide corruption-free rule and take care of the basic needs of the people, wins.

Barack Obama vs. Hillary Clinton:
Hillary had a vision of the USA being the No. 1 country in the world

by far, desiring to decimate the influence of Russia. As Secretary of State, she publicly gloated over the capture and death of the Libyan strongman Gaddafi by the forces she supported. She had an authoritarian style of management.

Obama, on the other hand, was more of a world visionary, seeing the US being a moral leader of the world, spreading freedom and also prosperity for all countries, not for the US at the expense of the other countries. He was more a champion of the poor as was evident in his Obama Care Program. Hillary though was more of a Republican than a Democrat in her value systems.

13 LEADERSHIP AND TERRORISM

Besides the damage that terrorism causes, in terms of loss of life or property and other assets, the greatest damage it inflicts is fear. This, in turn, translates to enormous economic damage far greater than the damage to life, property, and assets. This happens due to panic to enhance protective security in the forms of detection devices, check posts, deployment of security  personnel, fences, cameras, enhanced personal screening, etc. The investments in these, along with the cost of time and deployment of personnel, are huge. Politicians seem to be left with little choice other than finding out the solution to the root cause of terrorism and understanding and addressing it. However, political positions once taken are not easily changed for fear of inviting a loss of credibility with the public and their own vote banks. Giving up some territory of a country to another or permitting secession or independence may be at the cost of economic loss or unpopularity because of emotional positions by people or the risk to their own people's security. National and geopolitical considerations come into play.

For business leaders, there are concerns about the loss of markets, customers, suppliers, and alliance partners. Emotional reactions within organizations can be quite charged depending on the issue and the critics or supporters of the terrorist acts. Some may see terrorism acts as a fight for a just cause and not an act of terrorism within not just organizations but across political party spectrums, communities within nations, and even across nations.

The current global crisis is a great testing time for global political leaders, to see how they handle the situation in their own countries and how cooperation takes place at a global level. This is particularly crucial, unlike global warming where there are uncertainties and differences, and the challenge is not here and now. The dialogue and cooperation that have been emerging will hopefully lead to the realization that there is just a single planet, as was mentioned by one of the earliest astronauts to go in space, who said from up there he could not see any national boundaries, but just a single Planet Earth.

So, whether it is pandemics, global warming, political differences, threats of wars, proliferation, and amassing of nuclear weapons, or wide disparities of income distribution, the world should unite as just humanity and live in cooperation, peace, and harmony.

14 LEADERSHIP AND CORRUPTION

The word *corruption* is derived from the Latin word *Corruptus* which means corrupted. It is the abuse of authority by those in the branches of power in the executive, legislature, or judiciary.

When and how do leaders or those in higher positions in public or private spheres turn corrupt for personal benefit? Corruption has been around in human life since the beginning of organized societies and has also been condemned in religious teaching, though it has been practised ironically even by those who run religious orders. It helps political leaders secure political control by bribing others or spending on elections and thus enables a perpetuation of power and authority. It also enables to secure military and security power to perpetuate power, thus monopolizing political power. This is possible when:

1. There is low political freedom and press freedom, or an honest fifth estate that is bribed or threatened
2. There is low transparency in public or even large private organizations
3. There are poor regulatory rules or fulfilment of these in place
4. There is a higher bureaucracy

When and why do educated, well-to-do, highly compensated, successful individuals in control of corporations resort to large-scale corruption for personal gain? Is it that there is no limit to human greed? Is it constant comparison with others who have more that instils the greed for more? Is it family demand for wealthier lifestyles, homes, jewels, and jets that does it?

Weak law and order, and the absence of an efficient, speedy, and fair legal system make for ease of corruption. Tolerance of the people towards corruption, and the lack of ethics and morals in the education system tend to make corruption systemic in societies.

15 LEADERSHIP AND EQ

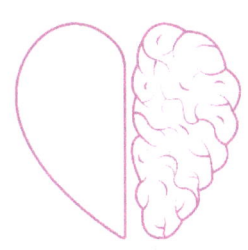

Emotional intelligence is a function of Emotional Quotient usually referred to as EQ. It is the part of the right brain that deals with emotions. A sharper development of that part results in a higher level of emotional intelligence and consequently greater awareness of emotions, thereby not allowing emotions to cloud decisions or behaviours. Thus, people can be both more sensitive and productive.

People with high levels of emotional intelligence are more resilient to change. They are more cooperative and open to others' viewpoints and are socially more active and involved. They are more in control of their behaviour. They handle adverse situations with a calm and thoughtful approach and have a lot of empathy. They have an optimistic outlook and focus on their centre of influence rather than their centre of concern. They hire teams beyond technical skills and look for skills that show signs of team empathy and teamwork.

Leaders with high emotional intelligence seek feedback, respect, and their team's ideas. They appreciate good contributions openly and frequently. They are aware of their limitations and do not hide them. They are self-motivated.

Research shows that the emotional hurt, stress, and depression of negative experiences fade over time. So, if one experiencing some negative feelings, it is useful to think of the Buddhist saying, *this too shall pass*. If one thinks of the experiences that happened a long time ago, it will feel less painful now than it was then. Time heals.

16 LEADERSHIP AND HAPPINESS

Living a balanced life is an important aspect to avoid the challenges of burnout, alcoholism, divorce, health issues, etc.

Many men feel that sacrificing family life and personal health is the price to pay for providing a better life for their families, especially if they did not enjoy the benefits of wealth and care from their father.

Women leaders, on the other hand, believe that family time is crucial for their children's well-being and for their children to see them as professionals who give inspiration, especially for daughters to pursue their own careers when they grow up.

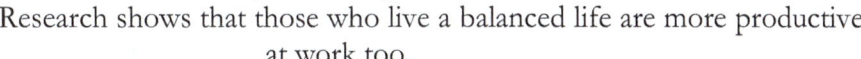

Don't squander health in search of wealth and end up in a hospital. Research shows that those who live a balanced life are more productive at work too.

The true goal of all leaders ought to be happiness creation and distribution for all the constituents and individuals of society with whom they connect. Leaders should endeavour to create a happiness index, not unlike the happiness index of nations such as Bhutan. Such indices do not believe that GDP and related financial indicators are a true measure of the well-being of the people belonging to a nation. They believe monetary measures do not indicate happiness. In fact, unhappiness quite often in the pursuit of wealth often leads to corruption, dishonesty, rivalry, inequality, wars, disease and depression.

17 LEADERSHIP AND LUCK

"The harder I work, the luckier I get" is the quote of Samuel Goldwyn, the famous film producer. So, is it just hard work that makes for success? Luck is defined as success or failure by chance and not by any actions. Seemingly, luck can contribute to one's success or failure.

Let's look at a few scenarios where it may be so. In a bureaucratic government, organization may be based purely on age or seniority. Hence, one may not be destined for a promotion. But if the person above suddenly quits or is fired or passes away, one may get the promotion or next higher position due to such an occurrence. Someone else's bad luck may be one's good luck.

If one is running a business that entails imports of some raw materials that attract duties, the government may change on account of global or bilateral trade agreements or need to encourage the increase of the production or reduce pricing of the product or may waive or withdraw duties. This results in a stroke of luck for the importing user, resulting in windfall profits as costs get reduced, or there is an increase in demand due to the ability to reduce prices.

Likewise, if a competitor has a sudden calamity of a natural disaster, it may be to the advantage of competitors to sell more or increase prices if there is a great deal of demand. So again, someone's bad luck can be someone else's good luck.

Unusual technological developments can be a lucky break for some. The recent breakthroughs in the internet and telecom technologies have been a boon for companies compelled to travel long distances for

meetings or courier letters back and forth by snail mail now possible via email and other forms such as Skype, Zoom, etc. The 9/11 attack on the World Trade Centre, insensitive as it may sound, was a lucky break for the manufacturers of security and surveillance equipment and systems, making their business boom. Of course, competition soon jumps in, and the lucky break may not last forever. Thus, besides being lucky with buying a lottery ticket, circumstances can give a helping hand. So, while hard work and diligence are crucial, one can get a lucky break from unknown quarters.

18 HUMOUR IN LEADERSHIP

Authors like Millicent Abel, Owen Hanley, and others have written about the benefits of humour. Adding a touch of humour lightens the mood at meetings. Laughter is indeed the best medicine as it releases endorphins which boost happiness. On top of these benefits, laughter also burns calories. According to one study, laughing 100 times burns roughly as many calories as 10 minutes on a stationary bicycle. The study also found that the average adult laughs 300 to 500 times per day. According to a Robert Half survey, 91% of executives believe a sense of humour is important for career advancement and 84% feel that people with a good sense of humour do a better job. Still, a Gallup study shows that we laugh significantly less on weekdays than we do on weekends.

The Bell Leadership Institute has found in a study that a high work ethic and humour are keystones to success. Harvard, MIT, and London Business School have also found that humour is an invaluable trait for successful leaders.

Humour at work is one of the best tools of emotional intelligence. It can be an ice breaker or a stress buster at work since most work situations are fraught with stress. Laughter and humour also promote better health as a result of reducing stress. It fosters teamwork, boosts productivity, and lowers absenteeism at work. It also boosts creativity and, thus, helps the bottom line in many ways.

When friends gather for an evening together they often share jokes, which creates a sense of bonding. The same is true of the workplace. It reverses the 'pratfall effect' which is that people feel more distanced from those who look perfect and superior. Hence, humour makes them look more normal and hence, likable. Humour also makes a public speaker speaking on a serious subject, more remembered.

How can organizations and leaders get their employees to laugh more? Since humour is subjective, what one may find amusing, another might find offensive or boring. The authors of two books on the subject—The *Humour* Code: A Global Search for What Makes Things Funny and Inside Jokes: Using *Humour* to Reverse-Engineer the Mind—believe that there's a formula for what makes all people laugh. The authors explain that humour rests on "benign violation"—that is, something provokes laughter when it is "wrong, unsettling, or threatening" but also seems "okay, acceptable, or safe."

The authors behind Inside Jokes—Matthew M. Hurley, of Indiana University; Daniel C. Dennett, of Tufts; and Reginald B. Adams Jr., of Pennsylvania State University—believe that we laugh when we find that something we've momentarily believed to be the case isn't in fact true, and at others in the same predicament, and at stories about such situations, especially if they are linked to pleasures of other kinds, such as insight, schadenfreude, superiority, etc. The simplest examples are puns and pranks.

Humour makes work more enjoyable. Hence, leaders can adjust their leadership styles and use emotional intelligence to be more empathetic, bond with colleagues over similarities and allow appropriate space for humour to add a bit of levity to the workspace. Fun team-bonding games also help as icebreakers.

19 PERSONAL AND PROFESSIONAL LIFE OF LEADERS

Can leaders have dual personalities like Dr. Jekyll and Mr. Hyde? If not, a big contrast or a wide variation in home behaviour and office behaviour? Can a strict parent be an empathetic boss?

We all live one life. While we can choose the people in our personal lives to a large extent, we cannot choose our parents or relatives. But we can choose our friends, our neighbourhood, and the people we connect with in our areas of personal interest such as sports, arts, or hobbies. In our professional lives, we have much less choice if we have a job. We cannot decide who our boss is, or who works with us, or whom we work with as colleagues or teammates. But we can choose where we work and change jobs or even professions if the work situation is not comfortable and conflicts with our values, attitudes, or behaviours. This may not be so easy in poor economic times. But it is perhaps better to be paid less, rather than work where one is in conflict with one's personality or values. Thus, leaders need to ensure that their own lives at home and at work are in harmony. Perfection may be a fantasy, but one can do one's best. Leaders are also obliged to try and have harmonious teams as this also results in higher productivity.

Research shows that those who live a balanced life (work, family, and health) are more productive at work and are happier too. If you're healthy and energetic, the business will be healthy and robust as well. Burnt-out teams do not generate the best results and can become resentful. Fatigue and stress significantly affect how well our bodies and brains function. Cultivating a work environment in which work-life balance is the norm can increase retention and minimise turnover and absenteeism. Furthermore, work-life balance generates a positive work culture and enhances brand perception.

Balanced leaders are able to delegate more, rather than racing to answer questions, email, and meet with clients in five minutes or less. They are more thoughtful in their decision-making and are more effective in their ability to lead. Their employees are more committed to the company because they know they make a difference. Leadership will thrive once the owner/parent/wife recognizes the correspondence between work, their personal life, and the mission of their company. This recognition and making a strong effort to achieve balance in these three life areas is imperative for leading a fulfilling life. If you sell your soul to the company, at the end of the day it is likely to fall apart. Leaders should not only strive to live balanced lives just for themselves but also strive to help those in their organizations live a balanced life.

The key to establishing an enhanced work-life balance is developing the right mindset. One needs to view their personal time at home as equally important as their time and role at work. Achieving a healthy work-life balance would require managing your professional and personal life in sustainable ways. Analyzing your present situation is the beginning step in achieving a balanced life. Keep a time log of everything, including work-related and personal activities. This data will serve as an eye-opener, helping you understand how you are using your time. Spend some time seriously reflecting on what is most important to you and make a list of your top priorities at work and at home. Then analyze your time audit by asking yourself what you need to start or stop doing, or continue doing, or do more or less of.

Incorporate mindfulness practices into your daily routine. One of the biggest causes of stress is ruminating, or repeating a certain stressful thought where the brain engages in an old thinking pattern and stays there. Mindfulness meditation re-grooves the brain and builds a new neurological network. Which helps one to stay calm and composed in the face of difficulties or stress.

Set fair and realistic limits on what you will and will not do both at work and at home. Clearly communicate these boundaries to your supervisor, coworkers, partner, and family. In today's digital world, while we are fortunate to have technology, it can also be a curse. Work-life balance goes for a toss when one becomes instantly accessible to anyone at any given time. This is where one should draw boundaries and not allow technology to control their lives and overwhelm them.

Focus 70% + of your time on High-Value Activities (HVAs), i.e., tasks that you are energized by and add the most value to the organization. Keep other distracting tasks at bay by tracking your HVAs and Low-Value Activities (LVAs). Effective delegation increases the amount of time that you will have to focus on the items that will move the needle.

Your health should always be your No. 1 priority. While you may not think you have time to add exercise and extra sleep to your jam-packed schedule, these practices relieve stress, raise your energy level, increase your stamina, improve your mental clarity, boost your immune system, and make you a happier, more engaged, and more productive person.

If your job or career is damaging your personal relationships, both areas will ultimately suffer. By making your personal relationships a priority, your productivity and effectiveness on the job will actually increase. It is also important to take some uninterrupted "you time" and indulge in some small pleasure daily. Setting aside a weekly day of rest can be helpful, as well.

If you are overwhelmed at work, and it is causing undue stress, know when to ask for help. Shed the Superwoman/Superman image and explain your situation to your boss or supervisor. Untenable work situations can usually be alleviated, but it will take some assertiveness on your part. Similarly, if a balanced life continues to elude you, or you are experiencing chronic stress, talk with a professional -- a counsellor, mental health worker, or clergyperson.

Take advantage of the services offered by your employee assistance program.

Today, Many forward-thinking companies are creating policies and programs that facilitate work-life balance. For instance, companies like Google provide recreation facilities, crèches, gyms, and nap rooms for their staff to balance life, be healthier, and also save on commuting time.

20 WHY LEADERS FAIL

Clear articulation of the organization's vision is a must-have for a leader. When a CEO takes over an existing organization, they need to confirm if they are in sync with the vision and mission of the organization. They also need to reconfirm with the key team members. Likewise, for a start-up, it is important to arrive at it with the participation of the key team members in formal and informal sessions. So, there is a clear buy-in all-round and a common purpose is arrived at. When this is not done it results in a disjointed beginning, and results in failure.

From the vision and mission, clear goals should be arrived at. From five years down to annual to monthly, for the first or next year going forward. So, failure to get team participation from vision and mission to goal-setting results in a bad start and the beginnings of failure.

Not being able to communicate all the way to the lowest levels is another recipe for failure. Frequent, monthly messages sent to the team highlighting success, failure, and challenges, help to give a sense of participation and commitment to the cause. Inviting suggestions from even unrelated areas and functions of the origination can result in some good ideas and suggestions from the most unexcited quarters.

Communication is not just about speaking but more about listening and also about getting feedback. This can be in the form of suggestion

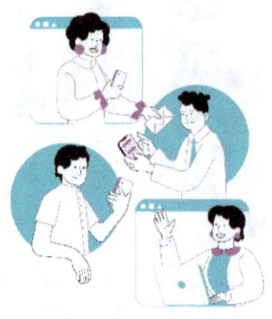

boxes, or real or virtual informal coffee break discussions. CEOs who walk about, succeed more than those who stay put.

Interpersonal skills should be practised since it creates a culture of better interaction and team bonding, and better efficiency and productivity. Poor interpersonal relations results in failures.

Unwillingness to face reality, especially in times of adversity, increases the level of failure. Facing reality in such times is the starting point to finding solutions, to the challenges being faced. Sharing them publicly is better than hiding them, as they will surface anyway and may also result in rumours spreading and an exaggeration of the challenges getting perceived.

Unwillingness to accept that the buck stops here and take responsibility does not augur well for creating a culture of accountability. Lack of clear goals, authority, and accountability results in failure.

Failure to delegate is a fatal flaw as it is the team that helps a leader succeed. So, it is crucial to train, develop and delegate. Training and creating a culture of learning ensure success. Not investing time and money in training results in failure, especially in the rapidly changing world.

Adaptation is the key to facing the changes in the environment. A wise leader adapts to circumstances like water adapts to the vessel that contains it.

In a world driven by quarterly successes, a need to meet stock prices, and rise above expectations, has resulted in leaders driving for results at any cost. The result is burnout, attrition, and eventual failure. So, driving people with no concern for their health, family life, or any aspect of their well-being results in failed leaders.

Unwilling to let go of control and not develop or delegate is the recipe for failure even if for some years success happens because of the drive. Leaders who lack the interest, ability, or understanding of people's development eventually fail.

Leaders who fail to embrace failure, fail in the long run. Failures are the stepping stones to success. Thus, risk-taking with the possibility of failure is a need for success. Investing in new ideas, products or services is the hallmark of success.

Leaders who do not acknowledge and reward the contribution of individuals, do not succeed. Recognizing and rewarding individuals for their hard work results in increased motivation and further success for the organization.

21 LEADERSHIP LESSONS FROM THE ANIMAL KINGDOM

Jennifer Smith of Mills College, and several scientists, anthropologists, and sociologists have carried out interesting research on leadership amongst animals.

"While previous work has typically started with the premise that leadership is somehow intrinsically different or more complex in humans than in other mammals, we started without a perceived notion about whether this should be the case," said Jennifer Smith in Oakland, California. *"By approaching this problem with an open mind and by developing comparable measures to compare vastly different societies, we revealed more similarities than previously appreciated between leadership in humans and non-humans."*

Amongst elephants, the seniormost matriarch is the respected leader, and as she ages and slows down, there is a natural succession when the next seniormost takes over. Among lions, the male lion leader is respected and followed as he provides security and protection for the group. The eagle flies high to get a vantage point view to see the whole picture. Migratory animals and birds signal with noise and indicate with noises about direction, food resources, and stops.

In most animal species, leadership has to be earned. Fought for first, then earned by providing security and food for the group as in lions, thus fighting their way to leadership and then earning respect. They breed and care for the newborn cooperatively and hunt and share with their pride.

Leopards have agility, speed, and stealth, and can hunt on the ground and up in trees. The gaggling of geese is to attract attraction and divert opponents. They fly in formation with a rotating leader in front. Penguins are capable of pushing a fellow penguin off a cliff to test if the water below is too cold to survive. If the pushed penguin seems ok, the others jump in.

Chimpanzees travel together, capuchins cooperate in fights, and spotted hyenas cooperate in hunting, but the common ways that leaders promote those collective actions have remained mysterious, Smith and her colleagues say. It wasn't clear just how much human leaders living in small-scale societies have in common with those in other mammalian societies either.

To consider this issue, a group of biologists, anthropologists, mathematicians, and psychologists gathered at the National Institute for Mathematical and Biological Synthesis. These experts reviewed the evidence for leadership in four domains—movement, food acquisition, within-group conflict mediation, and between-group interactions—to categorize patterns of leadership in five dimensions: distribution across individuals, emergence (achieved versus inherited), power, relative payoff to leadership, and generality across domains.

What Animals Tell Us About Female Leadership

As humans puzzle over the glass ceiling and how to get more women into leadership, could it be possible to learn something from the outliers of the animal kingdom? It's a controversial idea, but according to the scientists who made this discovery, the answer is yes.

Wild Styles

In a Mills College paper, animal behaviour professor Jennifer Smith and three colleagues identified eight species that exemplify female leadership: hyenas, killer whales, lions, spotted hyenas, bonobos, lemurs, and elephants.

To find this group, the team first had to pinpoint the social species that showed any leadership traits at all. By looking at things like movement, foraging, or conflict resolution, they identified 76 such mammals. Then within that group, the team searched for evidence of female leadership, and for the characteristics which define these female leaders.

"I think there's a lot to learn from these non-human societies," Smith says.

The researchers note it's important to not confuse leadership with dominance. "Leadership is something that happens because there is a problem that needs to be solved by some kind of coordinated action," says co-author Mark van Vugt, an evolutionary psychology professor at VU University Amsterdam.

Examples of problem-solving might be finding food, avoiding predators, or resolving conflict. Dominance, on the other hand, has more to do with competition between individuals. By the scientists' definition, successful leaders have willing followers—they don't need to convince people to join them.

Making Love, Not War

A whopping 99% of our human DNA is the same as that of our closest primate cousins—chimps and bonobos. But while chimps tend to be male-led, bonobos take their lead from females. Females make the travel plans, explains Takeshi Furuichi at Kyoto University, who studies bonobos in the Democratic Republic of Congo. Females eat first because they organise dinner.

Conflict is much less common in bonobo societies versus their scrappy chimp cousins. Female bonobo bosses, although smaller than males, regularly intervene as peacekeepers. While females often lose one-on-one scuffles with males, *"When more than two females collaborate (to fight) males, 100% of the time, females win,"* he says.

But given the choice, it seems bonobos would rather make love, not war. Intimate contact is common, and bonobo females use frequent sex to reduce tensions with both males and females. With females at the helm, bonobo society is a lot more chilled out.

Female bonobos can team up to overcome aggressive males—but are more inclined to be lovers, not fighters.

Matrilineal Elephants

In elephant families and orca whale pods, older females run the show. Wise orca grandmothers help their extended family thrive by knowing where the salmon are. When it comes to elephant leadership, *"We know that elephants have really good memories for patchy resources,"* says Vicki Fishlock, a scientist at Amboseli Trust for Elephants in Kenya. It is knowledgeable matriarchs that lead groups to water in a drought.

But when it comes to elephants, there's an important difference between us and them. Most human societies are patrilineal, with wealth and status passing down the male line. Elephants (and orcas) are matrilineal. *"Elephant females are born to leadership,"* says Cynthia Moss, director and founder of Amboseli Trust for Elephants, who has been studying them since the 1970s. In adult female elephants, "there is no choice, nor is there any struggle with males for position. Males live separately and do not serve as leaders among the family groups of elephants," she explains.

Calling the Shots

Hyenas are cooperative hunters. In hunting, mainly males lead. But in other ways, females call the shots. Female hyenas are larger and stronger than males, and direct where the groups go. Typically, hungry lactating females take the lead, followed by youngsters and males. Female hyena leadership is important during clan wars, when groups battle it out, usually over territory.

When female hyenas sniff each other's anogenital regions—a risky business for animals with such lethal jaws—it's analogous to a hug, explains Smith. After confirming trustworthy alliances, females join forces in another potentially risky behaviour: an attack. But female hyenas lead not only in battle but in defusing conflict within clans too.

So, while greeting your colleagues in a similar way to hyenas and bonobos may be off the cards, sussing out allegiances could be absolutely vital. One take-home message that can be drawn from analysing female leadership in mammals is the crucial importance of coalitions: whom you're friends with in your social networks and the expertise that comes with age and experience.

Female leadership, the animal world suggests, is more likely to emerge when females form cooperative units. Smith cites the #MeToo movement, as a parallel human example, where *"anyone can get involved, and it doesn't matter how much brute force you have,"* says Smith. These virtual coalitions of women forming *"are really influencing societal outcomes, so that is leadership, and that directly speaks to what we see in bonobos, hyenas, and these groups that join forces,"* she says.

But is it valid to make this leap from furry animals to working women? The idea is contentious, acknowledge Smith and colleagues. It's problematic because *"the level of complexity, and the differences in the social systems, is so great,"* says Christos Ioannou at the University of Bristol. *"It's such a big jump, that I think it's very difficult to make those comparisons,"* says Ioannou, who studies collective behaviour and leadership.

Smith's team argues that some forms of female leadership have been entirely overlooked. Leadership research often focuses on large, complex hierarchies within a business, government, or military. But the way some forms of female leadership work, within families and small groups, for instance, is more subtle but nevertheless provides valuable insight.

Even in primates with male-biased leadership, female leadership can go unnoticed. Julie Teichroeb, University of Toronto primate behavioural ecologist, studies vervet monkeys. Because females of this species lead from the middle or rear of a group—think middle management—early studies mistakenly determined that decision-making was done by large males at the front, she explains.

Of course, our biological legacy is only one aspect of why females are underrepresented in leadership. The other aspect is culture. People are skilled in cultural innovations that can change our own environment; therefore, Smith's teams argue that we could shape a future with more leadership opportunities for women.

The study provides more interesting ideas than hard evidence, but the authors plan more rigorous quantitative analyses in the future. Nevertheless, these eight species with strong female leadership suggest tantalising areas for further study.

Despite what those ongoing presidential primaries might lead one to think, the analysis by the scientific experts finds that leadership is generally achieved as individuals gain experience, in both humans and non-humans. There are notable exceptions to this rule: leadership is inherited rather than gained through experience among spotted hyenas and the Nootka, a Native Canadian tribe on the northwest coast of North America.

In comparison to other mammal species, human leaders aren't so powerful after all. Leadership amongst other mammalian species tends to be more concentrated, with leaders that wield more power over the group.

Smith says the similarities probably reflect shared cognitive mechanisms governing dominance and subordination, alliance formation, and decision-making—humans are mammals after all. The differences may be explained in part by humans' tendency to take on more specialized roles within society.

"Even in the least complex human societies, the scale of collective action is greater and presumably more critical for survival and reproduction than in most other mammalian societies," Smith said.

In Chinese culture, animals have great significance. An eagle represents far-sighted vision, wide perspectives, and dreams. The tiger fiercely protects his mates, children, and followers. Hence the tiger is seen as a guard or a protector, hence tiger statues at the entrance of houses in Chinese homes. Wild horses are hard to tame but very valuable and useful when one has done that. Like the team member who when guided can deliver great results to an organization. Horses because of their physical form are balanced creatures so one learns the importance of being balanced in life to succeed. Paintings of running horses represent strength, growth, and success in Chinese culture. Cranes are very flexible in their eating habits for survival, eating plants, insects, and small animals like rats too. They also use their long legs and necks to their advantage of long reach. In Chinese and other Eastern cultures, they represent longevity and wisdom.

While the tortoise is known to live long, it is slow and steady and hence wins the race of life, as do businesses that are patient though slow, and develop a hard shell to face adversity like the tortoise. The monkey's agility to spring from tree to tree and survive in any environment is an admirable capability. It shows how leaders can adapt to circumstances to survive and thrive.

Great leaders:
1. Manage effectively = Monkeys
2. Take an overview = Giraffes
3. Share Information = Lions
4. Empower through delegation = Wolves
5. Adopt a flexible leadership style = Leopards
6. Adapt to survive = All of the examples above

LEADERSHIP: THE PAST, THE PRESENT, & THE FUTURE

Some interesting leadership practices from animal species are mentioned below:

1. The Meerkat – stop running, pop your head up, look around, adjust course, then keep going. To maximise the chances of meeting our goals, we want to stay as close to the optimal path as possible. So, remember to be a little bit more like a Meerkat.

2. The Bee – create autonomy and empowerment to enable your team to work efficiently without a centralised leader. Successful teams share lots with a beehive. Everybody knows their role and can work independently.

3. The Elephant – create a healthy and safe environment for your team to ensure ongoing success and productivity. Your goal as the leader is to establish productive teams, who deliver consistently over a long period. And you need to be its team leader.

4. The Octopus – adapt your leadership style to each unique situation. No single way to lead is always right. A core skill any successful, modern leader needs to have at their disposal is situational leadership.

5. The Crow – develop and grow those around you

in a consistent and systematic way. Making sure everybody learns as much and as often as possible, gives them the best chance of reaching their career and personal goals.

6. The Dog – setting clear expectations removes ambiguity and enables valuable feedback. Be a master at setting expectations, especially for your team and peers.

7. The Gorilla – feedback is the most important tool for a leader to help others grow. Make sure you get good at giving feedback. Just like gorillas beating their chest.

22 THE NEW PSYCHOLOGY OF LEADERSHIP

Recent research in psychology points to secrets of effective leadership that radically challenge conventional wisdom.

Leadership styles have moved from the charismatic, based on Max Webber's description over a hundred years, when a leader was a driver, autocratic, charismatic, driven by a vision and goal that he goaded his people or team's work towards. Such leaders mentioned at the beginning of this book drove armies to conquest or destruction or their own ruin.

Political leaders have used the 'branding' identifying route to connect with their people. Some examples are Yaseer Arafat of Palestine's head scarf, Bush's leather jacket and cowboy boots, Gandhi's dhoti, and Jinnah's attire from different parts of the country.

This was followed by the business world at the beginning of the industrial revolution when there was little choice for the labour class trying to eke out a living. The world has come a long way and behavioural science has taught a lot about the human brain, emotions, rationality, bias, fear, stress, and happiness. So, humans can be treated like machines up to a point.

When their survival is at stake, they will do whatever it takes to stay alive. When that is not so, they need more than just food, clothing, and shelter to do their best. To be productive, creative, caring and cooperative with team members, they need positive feedback, recognition, freedom, flexibility, empathy, and

opportunities to be their best. So, from a driving, tyrannical boss telling them what to do, they need a manager asking them what they wish to do and what he can do to help. They need a leader who is willing to put his shoulder to the wheel with them, mentor and guide them, and help them develop and flourish as they work hard and help the organization flourish in turn.

Rethinking the Psychology of Leadership from Personal Identity to Social Identity

"I am, if I am anything, an American. I am an American from the crown of my head to the soles of my feet."

– Theodore Roosevelt

Since leadership is an influence process that focuses on group members being motivated to reach collective goals, leadership is ultimately proven by followership. However, this is something that classical and contemporary approaches struggle to explain since they centre on the characteristics of leaders as individuals. To address this issue, researchers have outlined a social identity approach that explains leadership as a process grounded in an internalized sense of shared group membership that binds leaders and followers to each other and is a basis for mutual influence and focused effort.

The question that lies at the core of the leadership process is – what allows the plans of an individual to be translated into the aims and desires of the masses? What is it that turns one person's vision into a collective mission that directs the energies of tens, thousands, or even millions of other people? The New Psychology of Leadership sets out an identity approach, which sees leadership as a group process that centres on a psychological bond between leaders and followers grounded in an internalized sense of their common group membership, that is, a sense of shared social identity.

Research shows that perceptions of charisma are critical to the leadership process. Reflecting on the Greek meaning of the word *charisma* as a "special gift", Michael Platow and his colleagues observe that leadership is best thought of as a gift that is bestowed on leaders, rather than one that is possessed by them. Thus, in bestowing charisma, followers also commit their energies to the leader. However, at different times and in different places, the same leader may be seen as more or less charismatic. This is because perceptions of charisma are a function of the changing social relationship between leaders and followers.

Transactional approaches view leadership as a form of social exchange in which followers work to realize a leader's vision to the extent they believe that the leader is working for them in return and that there is equity between what they put in and what they get out of the process. However, one of the key accomplishments of leadership is to transform the things we care about and make us concerned about things we previously ignored, whether that be particular commodities, equality, environmental sustainability, etc. Transactional approaches also miss out on the ability of leadership to transform followers' focus on individual benefit into a concern for the greater good.

On the other hand, transformational approaches state that effective leadership is based on more than just mercantile arrangements in which mutual obligation flows from interpersonal account-keeping. Instead, what makes the process remarkable is its ability to allow people to embrace a bigger vision of their place in the world, to work for the collective good, and thereby to scale new practical and moral heights. However, the limit of transformational leadership models is that they cannot fully deliver on their promise because they still do not fully break with psychological individualism.

What made leaders like Nelson Mandela and Theodore Roosevelt so effective was their sensitivity to social context. They envisioned and became emblematic of a particular group of people in a particular place at a particular point in time. This allowed them to transform the material landscape of society. This points to a simple yet fundamental observation – that leadership is not just about leaders and followers, but about leaders and followers within a specific social group.

Leadership Where Leaders are One Among Equals

There have been many studies and views on optimum leadership styles. Some studies have shown that circumstances of the organization call for a certain type of leader with certain qualities to successfully run an organization. Some believe that it is the leader who adapts to the circumstances of the organization and carries the team with him by the dint of his vision shared with the team and shared commitment to the goal of the organization. A symbiotic relationship between the leader and the team is what is called for in today's world connected via technology. It is an understanding of the new ethos of the younger generations.

Tajfel, Turner, and Bernard Bass of Birmingham University have shown studies in which optimum results occur when leaders establish to their teams that when their individual interests converge with group interests, the organization prospers. This is increasingly done through measures adopted by organizations such as stock options for employees and providing recreational, child-care, and fitness facilities at their place of work.

In certain situations, teams have found that being honest, trustworthy, humble, and open about their own weaknesses are more important than being brilliant and they foster greater commitment to the boss and organization. It has also been found by research that some organizations folded because the leaders received hefty remunerations even when the going was tough. Since the employees were aware of this vis-a-vis their own remuneration, they were put off by this and either quit or their productivity and commitment to the organization decreased. So down went the company but the boss walked off with a hefty package. Research also shows that leaders and followers must have a shared identity and vision.

Goals, Values, and Concepts

Leaders exert influence on the environment via three types of actions:
1. The goals and performance standards they establish
2. The values they establish for the organization
3. The business and people concept they establish

Successful organizations have leaders who set high standards and goals across the entire spectrum, such as strategies, market leadership, plans, meetings and presentations, productivity, quality, and reliability.

Values reflect the concern the organization has for its employees, customers, investors, vendors, and the surrounding community. These values define how business will be conducted.

Concepts define what products or services the organization will offer and the methods and processes for conducting business.

These goals, values, and concepts make up the organization's *personality* or how the organization is observed by both outsiders and insiders. This personality defines the roles, relationships, rewards, and rights that take place.

Roles and Relationships

Roles are the positions that are defined by a set of expectations about the behaviour of any job incumbent. Each role has a set of tasks and responsibilities that may or may not be spelled out. Roles have a powerful  effect on behaviour for several reasons like money being paid for the performance of the role, the prestige attached to a role, and a sense of accomplishment or challenge.

Relationships are determined by a role's tasks. While some tasks are performed alone, most are carried out in relationship with others. The tasks will determine whom the role-holder is required to interact with, how often, and towards what end. Normally the greater the interaction, the greater the liking. This in turn leads to more frequent interactions. In human behaviour — it's hard to like someone whom we have no contact with, and we tend to seek out those we like. People tend to do what they are rewarded for, and friendship is a powerful reward. Many tasks and behaviours that are associated with a role are brought about by these relationships. New tasks and behaviours are expected of the present role-holder because a strong relationship was developed in the past by either that role-holder or by a prior role-holder.

Culture and Climate

Culture and climate are two distinct forces that dictate how to act within an organization. Each organization has its own distinctive culture. It is a combination of the founders, past leadership, current leadership, crises, events, history, and size. This results in *rites*, i.e. the routines, rituals, and the "way we do things." These rites impact individual behaviour on what it takes to be in good standing (the norm) and direct the appropriate behaviour for each circumstance.

The climate is the feel of the organization, the individual, and the shared perceptions and attitudes of the organization's members. On the other hand, culture is the deeply rooted nature of the organization that is a result of long-held formal and informal systems, rules, traditions, and customs. This differs from climate, which is a short-term phenomenon created by the current leadership. Climate represents the beliefs about the "feel of the organization" by its members. This individual perception of the "feel of the organization" comes from what the people believe about the activities that occur in the organization. These activities influence both individual and team motivation and satisfaction, such as:

1. How well does the leader clarify the priorities and goals of the organization? What is expected of us?
2. What is the system of recognition, rewards, and punishments in the organization?
3. How competent are the leaders?
4. Are leaders free to make decisions?
5. What will happen if I make a mistake?

Organizational climate is directly related to the leadership and management style of the leader, based on the values, attributes, skills, and actions, as well as the priorities of the leader. Compare this to "ethical climate" — the feel of the organization about the activities that have ethical content or those aspects of the work environment that constitute ethical behaviour. The ethical climate is the feeling about whether we do things right, or the feeling of whether we behave the way we ought to behave. The behaviour (character) of the leader is the most important factor that influences the climate.

On the other hand, culture is a long-term, complex phenomenon. Culture represents the shared expectations and self-image of the organization. The mature values that create tradition or the "way we do things here." Things are done differently in every organization. The collective vision and common folklore that define the institution are a reflection of culture. Individual leaders cannot easily create or change culture because culture is a part of the organization. Culture influences the characteristics of the climate by its effect on the actions and thought processes of the leader. But everything you do as a leader will affect the climate of the organization.

Creativity

Creativity in a closed economy and low competitive environment was not considered important. But in today's rapidly-changing environment, it is crucial for organizations big, small, and even startups, to not only prosper but to even just survive.

The first priority of leadership is to get the right people involved at the appropriate time in creative work. That engagement starts when the leader begins to reconsider and recast the traditional roles of team members. It is crucial that employees contribute to the creative process and don't just mindlessly follow a new strategy that has been pushed on them. Al Kaltman said that successful leaders find ways to get normal people to perform at greater levels of efficiency.

The classic response to increased scale in an operation is increased reliance on process, standardisation, and continuous improvement. When organizations focus on process improvements too much, it hampers innovation over the long term. In creative work, one needs to have people exploring from different angles.

Make it Profitable

Few people have equal capabilities in idea generation and making it profitable; hence corporations normally separate the two functions. The consensus is that, eventually, an innovation reaches a point where it will be best served by people who know how to take it to market.

Limit the Bureaucracy

Executives must protect those doing creative work from a hostile environment. Managers must create the necessary structures to support cross-unit collaboration; they might unwittingly create other forms of bureaucracy.

Ideas and Levels

During an analysis of innovations at Google, its founders tracked the progress of ideas that they had backed versus ideas that had been executed in the ranks without support from management and discovered a higher success rate in the latter category.

Motivation

Motivating people to perform at their peak is especially vital in creative work. An employee uninspired to solve a problem is unlikely to come up with a novel solution. Employees doing creative work are more motivated by managerial behaviour, like a sincere word of public recognition than by monetary rewards.

Accept Failure

Any business that experiments vigorously will experience failure—which, when it happens, should improve creative problem-solving, team-learning and organizational performance.

When Anne Mulcahy was brought in to run Xerox, it was on the verge of bankruptcy. The first thing she did was acknowledge her limitations and then try and learn as fast as she could. She met and listened to dozens of employees, travelling at breakneck speed in the first few months. She raised capital and staved off bankruptcy. She cut operating and sales costs drastically, yet focused on innovation and new product creation. She pushed her team to their limits, winning their respect with her commitment and positive outlook. She even presented them with a vision plan, showing not what the company would achieve but as it was already achieved, instilling a visualization and affirmation for herself and her employees, and it worked. By 2003, Xerox made a profit of 91 million from losing 273 million in 2000 despite the competition from Japanese companies which had brought the company down. Profits rose to 859 million by 2006. She won over banks to restructure lending, got employees on her side, and got the technology engine running to keep pace with the Japanese. She consulted tech gurus and focused on the markets that had potential.

Leaders Need to Have Concern for Customers

When 9/11 struck, all airlines in the US were grounded. Passengers were stuck in different locations. Southwest Airlines, known for customer service, and James Parker encouraged staff all over the US to entertain stranded passengers at the company's cost and be empathetic to their circumstances. Three days later he announced no layoffs and, in fact, a profit share bonus for employees. Clearly, the airline's image and business soared.

Leaders Need to have Concern for their Own People

Henry Schultz of Starbucks flew to Washington DC to spend 3 days with the families of the 3 staff members who had been killed in a robbery. Starbucks' brand soared. Worldwide, a majority quit jobs because of poor relationships with their boss, resulting in high attrition, low morale, and low productivity.

23 EMERGING LEADERSHIP CHALLENGES

Among many leadership development challenges, the most notable are the barriers regarding:
1. Effective team development
2. Outdated leadership development approaches
3. Lack of evolving leaders' environmental perspective

But what if you can take it a step further by transforming leadership development with behavioural science? It makes sense to consider since it combines both psychology and economics to explore factors that can affect how well a leader is developed, including honesty, happiness, and value perception. Here's how:

Leaders should start by observing existing behaviour, then identifying where one is, and providing clarity on where one's reach is crucial for teams to buy in.

Take the case of the insurance startup, Lemonade. A customer of theirs, Brooklyn educator Brandon Pham, opened Lemonade's mobile app, signed an "honesty pledge" to attest to the truth of his claim, and then recorded a short video explaining that his Canada Goose parka, worth nearly $1,000, had been stolen.

That deceptively simple claims process is the by-product of academic research on psychology and behavioural economics conducted by Dan Ariely, one of the field's most prominent voices and Lemonade's chief behavioural officer. For example, Arely's work has demonstrated the power of priming—hence the very deliberate decision to have customers like Pham sign their name to a digital pledge of honesty at the start of the claims process, rather than at the end.

"There's a lot of science about when people behave and misbehave that has not been put to use," says Lemonade cofounder and CEO Daniel Schreiber. Some of that science would suggest design tweaks like signature placement. Other ideas are more fundamental to Lemonade's B Corp business model, like the decision to donate surplus premiums to charity. If customers are invited to direct leftover premium payments toward a non-profit of their choice, or so the thinking goes, they will be less likely to cheat on their claims (surveys suggest that 1 in 4 Americans would pay a claim with no compulsion).

Lemonade is even applying behavioural science to itself, publishing unusually transparent blog posts that include data on customer growth, bank account balances, and more. The posts bolster Lemonade's nice-guy reputation but also serve as a reminder that the New York-based company, which is currently licensed to sell rental and homeowner insurance, is still young and teeny-tiny, despite raising $60 million in venture funding. (Lemonade processed and paid out just six claims worth $4,589 in 2016, including Pham's.)

"They've raised a lot of capital, there are big expectations," says Nabil Meralli, a founding partner at London-based InsureTech Venture Partners. *"The potential and certainly the brand that is behind it have been strong."*

To succeed, Schreiber and co-founder Shai Wininger will have to scale a technology platform that is already leaps beyond the paper-pushing norm at industry stalwarts like Allstate and State Farm. But they will also have to prove that they can meaningfully lower customer acquisition costs and reduce fraud through the application of behavioural theories. Incumbents have history—and a $6 billion collective marketing budget. Lemonade has (experimental) science.

Uber talks of its determination to treat drivers more humanely. It is engaged in an extraordinary behind-the-scenes experiment in behavioural science to manipulate them in the service of its corporate growth — an effort whose dimensions became evident in interviews with several dozen current and former Uber officials, drivers, and social scientists, as well as a review of behavioural research. Uber's innovations reflect the changing ways companies are managing workers amid the rise of the

freelance-based "gig economy." Its drivers are officially independent business owners rather than traditional employees with set schedules. This allows Uber to minimize labour costs but means it cannot compel drivers to show up at a specific place and time. This lack of control can wreak havoc on a service whose goal is to seamlessly transport passengers whenever and wherever they want. Uber helps solve this fundamental problem by using psychological inducements and other techniques unearthed by social science to influence when, where, and how long drivers work. It's a quest for a perfectly efficient system: a balance between rider demand and driver supply at the lowest cost to passengers and the company. Employing hundreds of social scientists and data scientists, Uber has experimented with video game techniques, graphics, and non-cash rewards of little value that can prod drivers into working longer and harder — and sometimes at hours and locations that are less lucrative for them.

The Current Situation: Using the Same Methods

It is important to understand that the environment has changed. It is more complex, volatile, and unpredictable. The skills needed for leadership have also changed and more complex and adaptive thinking abilities are needed. But the methods being used to develop leaders have not changed much. The majority of managers are developed from on-the-job experiences, training, and coaching or mentoring. While these are all still important, leaders are no longer developing fast enough or in the right ways to match the new environment.

The Challenge Ahead: Developing the Right Mindset

This is no longer just a leadership challenge (what good leadership looks like); it is a developmental challenge (the process of how to grow "bigger" minds). Many managers have become experts on the "what" of leadership, but novices in the "how" of their own development and the development of their teams. This is where many programs and books fall short. Many  companies simply don't prioritize this effort or make a minimal investment of time and resources. Or they are investing in the wrong strategy.

The challenge is that existing leadership development strategies usually focus primarily on horizontal development: learning and developing skills and traits for "good" leadership. Practicing and improving things like good communication and emotional intelligence are imperative. But what is lacking is a focus on vertical development: evolving the way a leader thinks and views the environment around them. Simply focusing on horizontal development is like continually adding new software to an outdated computer. The returns are diminishing. When we upgrade to a new computer while also adding better software, we experience both horizontal and vertical development.

In combat or business, leaders with a higher level of cognitive development perform better in complex situations. They analyze data in a more sophisticated manner and therefore have the ability to make better decisions more quickly.

Cognitive development can be measured and elevated not only at the individual level but also across teams. Existing and emerging leaders within any type of organization must be given ownership over their development process. It must be an ongoing process and therefore the leaders must guide themselves through this journey.

The coronavirus has dramatically altered the world with a collapse of economies, and as a result, people have moved significantly to social distancing, wearing masks, and online for work, social connections, and food deliveries. Thus, some businesses such as health care, food production and delivery, sanitation, etc. have boomed, while some like travel and tourism almost completely collapsed for a while and are now recovering with the vaccines being available and a better understanding of care and treatment of the infected.

Corporate leaders should in times of crisis like the coronavirus crisis, get the entire team in the organization to buy in and get mobilized to handle the situation calmly, and in a spirit of cooperation and rise to the occasion as a team, for not just personal interest but also as a society that is being affected at a global level. It also calls for patience, and give and take among business partners, suppliers, vendors, and customers to overcome the crises and move ahead stronger than before.

24 LEADERSHIP CHALLENGES AND SOLUTIONS IN NON-PROFIT ORGANIZATIONS

Not-for-profit organizations face several challenges. The first one is the allocation of resources on overheads, some laws, and sometimes the guidelines set by donors, which limit the amount that can be spent on leadership development.

Like any for-profit company, non-profit companies too need the same approach to being successful. The demand for supporting various needs of society is increasing the need for philanthropic contributions. They need to develop fund-sourcing plans from philanthropists and effectively prepare 'marketing' presentations as slick as any corporate presentation, with audio-visuals, photographs, and 'testimonials' of delighted 'customers' to bring about emotional buy-in, for purse strings to be loosened.

Donors should use their expertise to help non-profits whom they fund, to handle the challenges in the following areas of leadership:

In the planning for both short term and long term – the plans should encompass human resource development, and training both at the site and in the office for the various support, admin, and field workers.

In building close long-term relationships amongst the teams working in the non-profit companies and the beneficiaries of the projects funded – they should be actively involved in jointly making decisions with the beneficiaries, to maximise the 'buy-in' and obtain active participation.

Diversity should be an important aspect of not-for-profit organizations. Diversity in sex, colour, nationality, age, etc. would contribute to building credibility with donors and the recipients of the projects where the funds are used. Diversity should be from the board level and at all levels.

Leaders can be developed from the recipients of the funds whose long-term commitment and hence knowledge from the beginning can add value to the non-profit organization and maximize the success of the ventures.

FUTURE

25 FUTURE CHALLENGES AND OPPORTUNITIES: THE WAY FORWARD

The traditional authoritarian approach to leadership no longer yields the kind of results necessary for business success. In fact, the behavioural approach to leadership has become a more effective way for business owners to relate to their employees and get the most out of their skills and talents. The behavioural approach to leadership focuses on the  human dimension of the workplace. By fostering an understanding of how people respond during times of conflict, and by teaching the best ways to manage expectations and motivate employees, the behavioural approach to leadership can help company leaders handle the varied human resource problems that occur during the workday. Understanding various behavioural leadership examples is the first step in implementing this approach.

There is also a need to learn from new behavioural science findings to prepare the workforce to face the challenges of the future as artificial intelligence begins to take over many human functions.

Leaders also need to figure out new ways to plan the structuring of remote teams working together. They need to learn how to leverage rapidly-enhancing technology to optimize the use of time, train talent, and optimize teamwork.

Professor Tom Griffiths of Princeton

University and founder of Hone Consultants has developed VILT (Virtual Instructor Led Training and Coaching). This is a combination of e-learning and online discussions. Yumi Kimura of Lead Consultants, specializing in human resources development, says balancing hard and soft skills will be needed for organizations to succeed.

Increasingly, it is becoming evident that soft skills such as creativity, empathy, interpersonal skills, social skills, and emotional intelligence which cannot be replaced by AI, will need to be developed. These are not yet given importance at present since the value of how much they can bring about greater success for organizations is unknown. This is borne out by Alexander Levitt, in his book, *How Humanity Works*, where he points out that such skills that are human and cannot be replaced by machines will be the competitive advantage that leaders in the Fourth Industrial Revolution will need to develop in order to succeed.

Sattar Bawany has coined the acronym VUCA (Volatile, Unpredictable, Complex, and Ambiguous) for the challenges faced by leaders due to the age of digital disruptions.

Countries are moving towards protectionism contrary to the spirit of the much-negotiated WTO treaty after years of negotiations, owing to the uncertainty of their country's future. Thus, the challenges of leaders both at the national and corporate levels are becoming increasingly difficult. A few global giants are beginning to assume monopolistic sway over business in all sectors of the economy, threatening the political independence of nations.

Radically new thinking and preparation are called for in the new industrial age, as the use and application of artificial intelligence, robotics, and digitization become more prevalent.

Klaus Schwab, founder of the World Economic Forum coined the term Fourth Industrial Revolution to describe the coming of the technology age, with the advent of the internet, mobile phones, and artificial intelligence.

It is crucial for leaders to embrace and apply technology to various aspects of business – be that accounting, marketing, manufacturing, human resources, using data analytics, robotics, and artificial intelligence.

A digitally connected world and the increasing uses of robotics and AI pose challenges and opportunities for businesses. The way forward involves collaboration, coopetition, innovation, creativity, and a greater focus on teamwork and team building, where the big boss is only one among equals. Younger people will actually be encouraged to be mentors to older people. So, future leaders will need to draw on all talent and subsume their own authority and ego, and share leadership with others. A cooperative leadership pattern needs to emerge.

Leaders in different areas of endeavour have demonstrated different leadership styles. Regardless of the style, some of the common features that are important for leaders and organizations in today's world are creating and communicating a vision, so that everyone is aware of the goals that will be achieved in the long run, and motivating people to make their contributions. Greater de-centralization of control and greater specialization could be key aspects of future organizations. Leaders will also keep adapting and evolving, possibly focusing more on mentoring, developing people, and strategizing, than on day-to-day operational management and administration.

Successful modern leaders understand that they are no longer a source of authority, issuing orders from on high. They are, instead, project managers, overseeing progress toward a goal and encouraging a team, however big or small, to move toward that goal.

Today, leaders want to get the most from their empowered workforce, are enthusiastic and energetic, persuasive, motivational, and collaborative – they seek input from their followers, are willing to change course if required, understand the importance of keeping their people informed, are willing to delegate while maintaining responsibility and are always open to learning.

Modern leaders are developed. They are constantly trained to improve their skills. Leadership skills can be taught; they are not divine gifts. However, an individual's personality comprising his or her family background, education, value systems imbibed, physical fitness, and well-being will inevitably have a bearing on an individual's leadership style. So, in a way, leaders are like all humans – the victims of their genes and environment – nature and nurture.

In the early times of emperors, kings, and invaders like Genghis Khan and Alexander the Great, sheer strength gave the leader the choice to do as he pleased, as during the Middle Ages. With the coming of the Industrial Age, it was circumstances, where individuals had little choice. Needing to move from farms to factories, they were at the mercy of the owners of factories or their managers whose key role was to extract the maximum from workers at the lowest possible cost to maximize profits for owners. Hence, an authoritarian dictatorial style was the order of the day. Irrespective of their own personality and inclinations, they had little choice to be different leaders. Even in today's environment of the need for empathy, fairness, freedom, and flexibility needed to retain people, the underlying driving forces are success and profits. What has changed is that people have more choices and hence these attitudes and behaviours are necessary. It is increasingly found that with dictatorial styles, there is high attrition, low buy-in to company objectives, and hence, higher possibilities of failure.

However, there are recent examples of leaders who have managed to be dictatorial and even insulting yet successful, offering youngsters chances and opportunities, unique learnings, and financial stock options, like Steve Jobs of Apple.

The coming world is fraught with dramatically new challenges for leaders. The head-hunters business is now booming. It is no longer easy to find internal potential promotion which is feasible to an extent. Nor is a quick LinkedIn search likely to find the match one is looking for easily. The challenges a CEO faces are many. They must be physically fit for long hours and extensive travel, and mentally fit to face media onslaught. They have to face super giants like Google, Amazon, Meta, and Microsoft, who are gobbling up more businesses. The developing world offers opportunities for new markets but needs to have CEOs who can handle the cultural, bureaucratic, and political manoeuvring often needed.

Cybercrime is a new, growing challenge. In the slow-moving world of the past, mainly focused on the manufacturing of steel, cars, chemicals, pharmaceuticals, and their ancillaries, the key was opportunity identification, allocation of resources, and diversification. The coming of the service sector boom and new tech computer hardware and software, both as businesses themselves and the opportunities and threats they present of losing out on the competitive edge by not being up to date, is looming large on a

daily basis. Cars, hotels, banks, and retailers are seeing the erosion of their physical strengths by the online world, with companies like Uber, Amazon, Airbnb, online banking, and yet more to come.

There is increasing pressure for CEOs to not just cater to shareholder interests but also be mindful of fairness to employees, suppliers, customers, and the environment, and yet be able to balance the books profitably.

Leaders of business, politics, and other fields will need to reflect and figure out ways to handle some of the macro challenges that are emerging, like the divergent pulls of globalization and nationalism where countries wish to export their goods and services while restricting imports to manage their balance of payments, imposing import restrictions and tariffs on imports, or forming regional or developing bilateral trade relations where mutually acceptable.

These challenges have also resulted in immigration concerns with immigrants being a burden on the economy and taking jobs away from nationals. They offer their services at a lower wage to meet their survival needs.

Given the terrorism concerns, they also give rise to fears (founded and unfounded), given that terrorism has resulted in far less damage than wars, both global and regional. This fear and threat have also given a boost to industries such as security businesses that manufacture scanners, cameras, etc. So, terrorism seems to serve its purpose by instilling fear and resulting in immense investments in security thus inflicting economic damage, far greater than the physical damage it has caused.

The environment is another area of huge emerging concern for leaders since ignoring it risks the survival of the planet itself. Some studies have shown that plastics that are causing untold damage to land, sea, humans, animals, and marine life can be economically harnessed, as most plastics are recyclable and reusable, except that it is a little more expensive than the extraction of fresh fossil fuels. So, the  suggestion is to create a fund to pay for the difference in cost as an environmental protection fund for recycling plastics and reducing the extent of fresh fossil fuels being extracted and also the need to harness solar, wind, and water energy, even if more expensive technology at this stage of extraction and recycling is needed.

The outbreak of diseases has impacted human life and thrown it out of gear at the national, global, and business levels. The plague in the 18th and 19th centuries and SARS in recent times, have spread panic and sent stock markets crashing.

War is another major cause of turmoil for humans. Though its immediate impact in regional wars is limited initially in the region concerned, it invariably has widespread consequences. It results in damage, death, disease, migration, poverty, and fear that have impacts far beyond the actual boundaries of the conflict.

So, awareness and being abreast of geopolitical developments beyond their own national boundaries is crucial for political and business leaders.

When the crowds where Christ was condemned to die asked the judge if it was true that Christ was guilty, *"What is truth?"* asked Justice Pilate and left without waiting for an answer. Fake news, as we call it today, and propaganda have been around for centuries. They have justified wars, conquests, occupations, and colonisations, from the Chinese emperors to the Russian Tsars, to the First and Second World Wars to current day 'democratic' election battles, to justifying laws on immigration to the US, India, and Europe.

Religion was extensively used to create myths and manipulate humans, be it the miracles of Jesus, Allah, Bhagwan, or the Jewish religious beliefs. Adam and Eve, and heaven and hell were created to hold sway over people.

So, fake news has been around for centuries to manipulate humans and make them act in a certain direction for the benefit of people who have a vested interest in their doing so, specifically the spread of exhortations by religious leaders to wage crusades by the Christian Church or Jihad by the Muslim clergy. So, millions can be manipulated to act and risk ruin or even death for a cause they are made to believe is greater than their survival. Often the fear this risk may arouse is allayed by the assurance of a better afterlife. Thus, the big emerging challenge is not just of fake news but the more insidious one of manipulation of the true with the untrue. So, fake news even at national levels has continued to be held and attempted to be perpetuated, like the denial of the existence of the Jews and Palestinians, and creating claims and selective historical or cultural information to justify the same.

With the advent of the internet, and more recently social media, fake news is the order of the day. Today it has taken ominous dimensions of fake news about disease, riots, and deaths, to try to win an election, support a cause, promote a commercial interest, spread panic and fear, or even use it merely as a bad joke.

So, to distinguish between truth and untruth, the best is to rely on credible sources of information, like research institutions, publications, and individuals of long-standing repute. This is easier said than done as all of us carry our biases. It may be more difficult to be biased on scientific data in areas like healthcare, or astronomy, but in the social sciences such as history, political science, economics, and especially religion, huge biases creep in.

Unfortunately, political leaders are spreading fake news, and are hiring professional firms to help them win elections or other causes. Cambridge Analytica, a firm that has helped electioneering by leveraging and planting true and fake news to help their clients, is a recent example of this. Some companies are also planting fake news about their competitor's products or services and broadcasting on social media any negative news about competitors that may be found in the media.

So, what should 'clean' political parties and business firms with high ethical standards do to cope with this? In the political arena, opposition  parties engage in a maligning competition. Business firms should publicise accurate information, maintain their ethical standards and refrain from countering this in the same manner and establish their integrity and authenticity by not doing so. In the medium to long term, truth prevails.

While there are advertising standards and regulations in many countries, there is no such regulation in the political free-for-all arena.

Hitler, in his book *Mein Kampf*, said that the best way of propaganda was to speak a lie repeatedly and it would be accepted. It does appear that some aggressive marketing campaigns seem to follow this approach. Even if they are not lying, they exaggerate the benefits of their products or services and publicise selective comparisons with competitors to highlight the superiority of their products or services. Although there do exist regulatory bodies to control this, there is often a thin dividing line between what is fair and unfair advertisement.

How Newly Virtual Leaders Can Succeed

Although technology has helped us work and communicate remotely, organizations have not yet mastered the art of leading virtual teams. For many, working from home and communicating via video conference platforms like WebEx, Zoom and Microsoft Teams are nothing new. However, leads need to pause and understand what they need to do differently in order to sustain smooth functioning in a virtual setting, especially at a time when their teams are looking to them for direction.

Working virtually does not come without its challenges. For some, it is uncomfortable to work from home, and this discomfort makes it harder for them to connect, trust, and communicate with their team members and leaders. Interpersonal dynamics are also harder to manage in a remote setting since it is more challenging to read peoples' body language over video. It is also difficult to engage people in virtual meetings.

Ask yourself these five questions to ensure that you're being a good virtual leader:
1. Am I being strategic enough?
2. Have I revamped communication plans for my direct team and organization at large?
3. How might I reset roles and responsibilities to help people to succeed?
4. Am I keeping my eye on and communicating about the big picture?
5. What more can I do to strengthen our company culture?

Top Challenges for Future Leaders

"A leader of the future will have to be astute enough to balance automation with the human touch. They have to decide what types of tasks to automate so that they can spend more time on high-value activities. But also decide which businesses will continue to benefit from human judgment."

— Kiran Mazumdar-Shaw, Chairperson, of Biocon

Future leaders must know how to strike the balance between investing in technology and focusing on their people to ensure success in the future. While most of us have been conditioned to think only of the short-term, future leaders need to be focused on long-term success and learn how to adapt to technology. The world is changing incredibly fast, and future leaders will be challenged to embrace change, stay agile, take risks, and absorb new ideas.

Technology is certainly important, but organizations cannot work without people. People are an organization's biggest asset. The challenges of humanizing involve balancing humans with technology and encouraging diverse teams to bring new perspectives to the workplace. people want to be part of organizations that care about more than just making money. Future leaders need to make sure their work is improving the world and then share that message with others.

Leadership and Transhumanism

Transhumanism is the physical merger in parts of biology and technology, i.e., the embedding of technological components/parts such as microchips, artificial limbs, and embedded circuitry in the brain to enhance, speed up or enable physical human movements or thoughts. The movement of artificial limbs or thoughts being manipulated by altering the brain could help autism or Alzheimer's Disease to be cured or managed better and could also help in enhancing human IQ.

How do leaders handle such developments or available technologies? If these could help enhance profits, would they use them indiscriminately? Would they pose moral dilemmas? Would regulatory laws be put in place? Playing God would not be easy for corporate or government leaders. When transhumanism moves more in the direction of Artificial Intelligence, many opportunities and challenges would arise. And they are already arising. With the advent of robots, humans are being robbed of jobs, so should the government regulate or ban these?

AI technologies, including OpenAI's ChatGPT and Google's Bard, have made a significant impact over the past year with their remarkably human-like responses and their capacity to generate content ranging from novels and poems to intricate computer code. Despite concerns from some leading industry executives about the potential elimination of approximately one-third of jobs due to these advancements, CP Gurnani, a veteran CEO in India's $245 billion information technology industry, maintains that skilled professionals will not be replaced.

There was huge resistance to the introduction of computers in organizations and especially government organizations. Trade unions went on strike, resisting their introduction. They were only allayed when training programs for the use of computers were introduced or alternate jobs were offered to those who could not adapt. Voluntary retirement options were introduced as well.

With the possibility of large-scale Artificial Intelligence replacing humans, ideas that humans will have more time for leisure to pursue arts, music, theatre, sports and pleasure activities are being seen as the possible bright side of such developments. But if these are to be available to the top bracket of the wealthy and the majority do not find alternate income or worthwhile pursuits, then it will result in social upheavals. To preclude this from happening, ideas of minimum basic income for all are being talked about.

Since AI can only draw conclusions on the basis of guidelines set and past data programmed, AI will need to seek it from humans if it is missing, or dish out wrong or inaccurate decisions.

26 APPLICATIONS OF BEHAVIOURAL SCIENCE AND TECHNOLOGY

It is not new news that a lot of what drives human behaviour is often unconscious and irrational. We go back to the end of the 19th century and find Sigmund Freud trying to describe our unconscious and intervene on at least what he thought was more or less a scientific basis.

The good news is that our understanding of the unconscious mind has come a long way, grounded in decades of basic research into what drives ordinary, everyday human behaviour. These are the biases, the heuristics, the rules of thumb that determine the great majority of our day-to-day decisions without us even being aware. So, yes, we can agree with Freud that we are often irrational, but as today's behavioural scientists like to say, we are predictably irrational. What can be predicted can be managed, at least to some degree.

Human psychology has been explored and used for management purposes for the past 100 years. Freud gave us a very deep insight into the human mind and how it works. The issue had always been, though, that while Freud's insights have been very useful, they have been very hard to implement because they were so deep and hard to grasp and alter.

Now we have the insights that people are predictably irrational, but we also have the tools coming out of it to help alter and guide behaviour. What we use is the insight not only from behavioural sciences but also from neurosciences, most recently.

The human brain is spectacular. At any point in time, over 11 million bits of information hit our brain, and it's able to filter them down to about 50 only. Then 7 to 10 of them can be kept in short-term memory. Of course, with this enormous filtering exercise that it does, we cannot consciously make choices all the time. A lot has to happen very unconsciously. And that's a very different unconscious from the unconscious that Freud has been talking about.

One of the main applications of behavioural science for companies is performance management. You can identify factors that actually hinder performance as well as those that foster it. Money is not always the best motivator. The second piece is recruiting and succession planning. Here, machine learning has a much stronger ability to predict future success than those that have  been, for example, choosing or selecting CVs in the past. And then at last: cultures, be it for merger management, or a general cultural change that you could see with bringing agility or more diversity to an institution, or something as targeted as introducing a safety culture, for example.

With nudges — subtle interventions based on insights from psychology and economics — we can influence people's behaviour without restricting it.

The general idea behind nudging as well as debiasing is that people are predictably irrational.

With a nudge, we could get people to do whatever is best for them, without prohibiting anything or imposing fines or restricting their behaviours in any other hard way. In terms of nudging, there are different applications for companies. One certainly is marketing, and marketers have been using similar approaches for a long period of time.

Nudging is much more a function of the behaviour that you'd like to see in your company, like something in line with your company values or what your company stands for. That's the decision executives have to make. Nudging is then merely a technique to make this behaviour more likely, but it's a choice of the behaviour that makes the difference.

Another area of application, in particular, is safety culture. In terms of irrational thinking, this is absolutely something irrational—to risk your life by not sticking to the procedures.

With behavioural science, companies are able to go away from the backward-looking approach, where after something happens, you try to understand what the reasons were and take them out, to something forward-looking, where you try to not attack people's mindsets but change the environment in a way that becomes simpler and more intuitive for people to follow safety procedures.

One of the problems that construction companies have is that managers, once they become promoted, stop wearing the helmet, as a sign of superiority to the workers. A nudge that's implemented by some companies is that the managers get a helmet of a different colour. They use the same status bias but in a different way to help people stick to safety procedures.

We're not always rational, and sometimes that rationality—or lack of rationality, rather—has a real impact on the decisions that we make. That can be extremely costly for organizations.

Understanding Human Behaviour

Behavioural science, positive psychology and neuroscience propose new ideas to hone skills and optimize performance in the workplace. Lee Newman, Ph.D. in Psychology and Computer Science from the University of Michigan, Dean of the IE School of Human Sciences and Technology, and Professor of Behavioural Science, Leadership, and Analytics, analyzes the two revolutions happening in the organizations today.

Why has understanding human behaviour become so important in business?

Understanding human behaviour and what we know from behavioural science is very important in many ways in business. One example is what we call "nudging," which is about designing small psychological pushes that guide people (employees, customers) toward desired behaviours. For example, some energy companies show you how your energy consumption compares to that of your neighbours on your monthly energy bill. If your energy consumption is higher than your neighbours', you get a sad face; if it is lower, you get a smiley face. A simple change in the graphics and information provided in the monthly energy bill—comparing people to their neighbours and adding a face—has been shown to positively affect how much energy people use. That's an example of how subtle psychological nudges can make a big difference in business.

Working with Biases

LEADERSHIP: THE PAST, THE PRESENT, & THE FUTURE

Leaders in the future have to be aware of biases and fight them. It starts with the recruiting processes, with the behavioural design of how to make them function in a way that doesn't favour those — we call it a "mini me" bias — who have always been recruited to the company before and would be recruited all the time. Because again, our human brain is biased, and we enjoy having those that remind us of ourselves, around. If one wants to have a diverse set of leaders in the future, they have to be aware of those little biases and fight them right at the start of the recruiting process.

In Germany, together with about 20 other companies, a research team worked on an initiative called Chefsache that wanted to bring more women into leadership positions and create gender balance. As one of the focus topics, they looked into unconscious bias within talent processes. When you look into recruiting, even with the best intentions, there was this mini-me bias. People make biased choices and might miss out on talent because of those.

One of the debiasing techniques that the research team used was that after they've seen a case and they have a team speak about what they've seen, they now never let the most senior person in the room speak first, because there's something called the "sunflower" bias, which means that once the sun speaks, the flower follows. This means that in the group, people would more likely adopt the senior person's position, maybe even a different position from the one that they had before, thereby sucking up to the boss!

Another intervention is to combat the bias that occurs—in recruiting, for example—called groupthink. You make people fill out a statement on the candidate themselves before they enter the group discussions, because science has also shown that once a group starts adopting a certain opinion, it's very hard for the individuals that haven't spoken yet to bring in another thought or have another opinion. There we'd say, never let the most senior person in the room speak first. Make sure that everyone notes the opinion right after having seen the recruitment candidate and before sharing their opinion.

Thinking Clearly under Pressure

One important finding from recent decades of behavioural science research is the surprisingly stark intellectual impairment that results when someone feels mildly threatened, even by "threats" that are distinctly existential rather than physical. Research has found that even low levels of negative stress seem to reduce activity in the brain's prefrontal cortex—the region responsible for reasoning and forward-thinking.

That's a big problem, given that the workplace is full of potential threats to people's sense of security, self-worth and social standing. After all, most of us have had moments when we feel out of our depth or underappreciated, and we've all seen people being talked over or even slapped down in meetings. These sorts of slights are small, but they can be enough to undermine anyone's sense of being competent, respected and in control—which means they're enough to reduce a person's cognitive capacity just at the point when they might want to be rising to a challenge. The good news is that once managers understand how hard it is for someone to think clearly and make good choices when something has put their brain on the defensive, they tend to take a more effective approach to handling tricky conversations with colleagues.

For example, imagine that a team leader has called a meeting to discuss a crisis at work—perhaps one of their company's self-driving trucks has crashed. The problem with this sort of situation is that it's hard for the people involved to avoid freaking out at least a little, and that anxiety means they won't be doing their best thinking about the solutions needed.

So, instead of leading with statements like: *"Okay guys, this is bad, we have to fix this,"* a leader with a basic understanding of behavioural science might have learned to deploy one or two positive framing questions to help get their colleagues off the defensive. For example, they might ask something like: *"When have we solved problems well in the past? And what does that tell us about what we might do now?"* Or: *"When we look back in a year's time, what will we be proud of having done in this moment?"* These sorts of questions aren't glossing over the problem. The team still needs to understand what has gone wrong. But by framing the problem in a way that re-injects a sense of possibility and purpose, a skilful leader can do a great deal to boost the collective IQ their team can bring to the table.

Resolving Workplace Disagreements

The same understanding of the human brain's "defensive mode" can help a manager better understand how to resolve workplace disagreements more effectively. If human workers are increasingly focusing their time on grey-area situations where there isn't one correct answer that can be computed by AI, it is fairly likely that there  will be differences of opinion between people working on a project. And the problem with disagreements is that when you're in the middle of them, it all too easily feels as if your perspective isn't getting a fair hearing—something that presents a pretty clear threat to the average brain. If either or both sides of the argument are in this defensive state of mind, intelligent debate is difficult.

Game theorist, Anatol Rapaport, developed a technique that neatly reduces the level of defensiveness on both sides, making it easier to resolve the dispute, and it isn't hard to learn.

Its power lies in the first two steps. First, you articulate your antagonist's perspective in a way that's as compelling and generous as possible. Then, you emphasize all the points where the two of you agree. After that, you go on to explore the remaining points on which you truly do disagree. By making people feel heard and reducing the sense of oppositional threat all around, the opening gambit has been found to make it far easier for both sides to think expansively and reach insight on the right way forward.

There are scores of techniques like these that emerge from behavioural science research and that are eminently teachable. Right now, behavioural science doesn't get much airtime in the average management training program or business school curriculum. But in the years to come, we are going to need all the help we can get to ensure that

 we excel at making the most of the soft machinery inside our heads.

Gallup's *State of the Global Workplace* study suggests that only 13% of employees worldwide feel actively engaged in their work. Most of the rest feel rather apathetic, but a significant number (24%) say they feel "actively disengaged" by their work. That may include your boss, by the way, since the numbers look just as bad for the category that Gallup calls "professional workers and managers/executives/officials."

Hence it's perhaps no surprise that people ask: *"All this advice on how to be at your best—I get it. But realistically, what can you do when you're surrounded by difficult people?"* The glib answer, of course, is: *"You should quit!"* But most people can't simply walk out of their jobs, at least not immediately. Moreover, it's not easy to make thoughtful, balanced career decisions when you're feeling desperate. So, while it's a good idea to work on an exit strategy if you're in a toxic place, it's also worth doing what you can to improve your daily experience right now—if nothing else, to help you think more clearly about your next move.

Human beings are wired to find it fundamentally satisfying and energizing to learn new things, even small things. Researchers have found that simply getting answers to questions is enough to activate the brain's reward system (something TV game show producers guessed a long time ago). And the truth is that even in the worst of situations, there is something to learn. You might decide: *"I'm going to learn how not to completely lose it when dealing with the office psychopath,"* and experiment with different techniques for staying calm under pressure until you become a master at it. Working with obstructive colleagues? You could decide to hone up on a range of influencing techniques. It's a good way of making you feel that your time isn't wasted. And if your goal becomes learning new things, even repeated failure becomes useful—because (paraphrasing Thomas Edison), you'll simply be learning what doesn't work. Just remember to take notes as you go along, to cement your learning and help you keep track of interesting stories you can tell in your next job interview.

Positive Leadership

Another important way that behavioural science shapes business is what we call "positive leadership." We know from hard science, and particularly the field of positive psychology, that people's daily emotions—the concrete, daily positives and negatives we all experience in a workday—can have a big impact on performance. For instance, we know that negative emotions we experience after a high-conflict meeting or when someone upsets us, can narrow our attention, making us less open to new or innovative ideas. At the same time, simply being in a negative emotional state can make us more likely to negatively misinterpret other people's behaviour or their intentions. On the other hand, when we experience positive emotions in the workplace, it can positively impact our behaviour. For example, people who are experiencing positive emotions after a great team brainstorming meeting or a big success with a client tend to be more open-minded in their thinking and more creative in finding solutions to problems. They tend to have what we call a "lower psychological distance" from other people. As a result, if there's a conflict or they're negotiating, they tend to find more common ground than when they're experiencing negative emotions. These are examples of how understanding positive psychology might help us better understand our own behavioural drivers and make changes in our daily experience to boost our productivity and effectiveness.

Combining Data Analytics with Behavioural Sciences

Why is it so important to combine data analytics with behavioural science when starting a business?

Evidence-based management and thinking don't use intuition but make analytical-oriented business decisions based on facts and data.

The way human beings choose to collect information, the way we analyze that information, and the way we make final judgments or decisions based on information, can be very biased. We can refer to well-known cognitive biases that people have studied, most famously, Daniel Kahneman, the psychologist who won the Nobel Prize in Economics in 2002. For example, research has shown that the moment we form an opinion or have an emerging mental proposal, we often unconsciously look for information that tends to support that opinion or proposal. We may evaluate neutral information in a way that we believe supports what we're thinking. That's one example of what we call "confirmation bias," but there are many such types of very unconscious biases.

When you move to a world where people are using data all the time to make decisions, it's very easy to forget that we as human beings are the ones who choose where to look for the data, how to collect and analyze it, how to visualize the data, and ultimately in most cases we make the final conclusions. So even though machines, computers, and algorithms are an increasingly important contributor to good decision-making, ultimately we have to understand some of the traps of human thinking when it comes to human decision-making and learn to avoid them. That's why it's important that people who are heavily involved in analytics and data-based decision-making also understand some of the psychological perils and traps involved.

Technology and Soft Skills

How might technology change the way we train workplace behaviours, particularly soft skills?

One example of new and interesting technologies that hold great promise for improving the effectiveness of how we train behaviours and soft skills in the workplace, comes from the world of digital media.

We now have technologies for immersing ourselves in virtual realities—digital or augmented—that combine the real world with the virtual world. These technologies are extremely interesting, and they are evolving in sophistication very quickly. One way to use them would be

in training communication skills. There are many training programs out there. You can read books on how to be a good speaker, how to be influential, how to give speeches or present information, or pitch a business idea to potential investors. You can read a lot about it – and, if you're lucky and someone pays to train you, you can give speeches or pitches in front of a coach or a small audience and get feedback from those people. But that's very expensive, and you can't do it frequently because it requires getting about 50 to 100 people in a room to listen to you, paying a coach and having someone there to evaluate your performance.

But now let's imagine you put on virtual reality glasses. Now you're immersed in an extremely realistic room of 400 people who are moving in their seats, checking their e-mail and their smartphones, rolling their eyes and yawning. You can imagine programming algorithmically specific behaviours to create a very engaged audience, a partially engaged

audience or a very disengaged audience. You, as the presenter, can then be in this virtual auditorium with those 400 people and try to give a good business presentation. While you're giving it, the virtual attendees of your presentation can actually react in real-time to what you're doing based on an algorithm. You might program them to be a difficult crowd, so that if you start to pause between sentences or use the word "um" too many times, the digital attendees will start to roll their eyes, get bored, check their telephones, and move around in their seats. That gives you instant feedback, which you can then use to adapt. We can create very realistic virtual realities, so that people can practice their presentation skills over and over again under different scenarios. You can even imagine those virtual spaces providing some kind of dashboard, where you have a set of meters showing you how engaged the audience is, or how much they are moving around. These devices could measure your heart rate, so you could be looking at 400 people in virtual reality and see whether your heart rate goes up or down. You could see whether you're moving your own body too much or too little. You could have a meter that measures the modulation of your voice. You might set a voice modulation objective, because maybe you're a person that's too monotone, and you need to learn to modulate your voice better. This way, you can watch the voice modulation meter as you're giving the presentation, and, if you're not up to a certain level, you can take immediate action to improve it.

You can imagine how someone could practice with this virtual audience and, in a very short time, actually build voice and bodily modulation habits and become a much more engaging speaker. This is one fairly detailed and concrete example of how digital media technology can be used to radically improve the effectiveness of soft skills training, in this case, for presentation skills. This is a radically higher ROI than anything possible now in verbal communications training.

Employee ID badges can measure people's communications in meetings and produce maps of the communication between employees: who's talking to whom, who's not talking to whom, tone of voice and so

on. This kind of technology can also help us develop more balanced communication skills for working with other people in meetings. Likewise, we will soon see wearable technology being able to measure our emotional arousal quite accurately. So, we can imagine seeing data from high-conflict situations and getting feedback on how well we are able to manage our emotions during difficult moments in a day at work. These are all examples of how technology, either by engaging people in virtual realities or measuring our behaviours, can give us much more feedback, more often, and at a much lower cost. We can then use this feedback to adapt our behaviours, practice new ones and get into more productive habits. This is called "behavioural fitness training".

In a certain sense, we are talking about networking with everyone, with the entirety of the things we are connecting with, to get feedback and information from everything. Some call it the Internet of Bodies (similar to "the Internet of Things"). We are augmenting our bodies with devices and connecting ourselves to our cars, our bed, our refrigerator, etc. to obtain an integrated system for managing ourselves as bodies.

Technology, either by engaging people in virtual realities or by measuring our behaviours, can give us much more feedback, more often, and at a much lower cost.

The personal learning cloud is a depository of online courses with content available from LinkedIn Learning, Skillsoft, Salesforce, and others. These offer online interactive soft skill courses on demand, thus taking soft skill learning to a new level outside the meeting room and into the virtual environment. These courses can be part of a training schedule or program for corporate executives, or as a self-development option for individuals for specific professional skills development needs or personal development enhancement.  They can be paced as needed, as per the needs of the organization or the individual, thus being useful for recruitment, training or promotions needs for organizations and individuals.

People who work in teams can form groups to learn in, thus enabling the social interactions as would be possible in a classroom/meeting room environment. The learning results can be tracked at an organization or individual level, so keeping track of progress is possible.

So, certifications in specific streams or areas can be developed, saving the need for broad-based MBA degrees and other expensive training programs which are often not needed in on-the-job situations in many instances. So, customised qualifications and topic-specific mini certifications are possible, thus enabling enormous cost-savings, including cost efficiencies of travel, hotels, etc. Companies and individuals can be more conscious of enhancing their competitive advantage via cost-effective customised training and learning. This also offers possibilities of measuring ROI on recruitment training and development.

Big Data, Advanced Analytics, Machine Learning and Behavioural Science Knowledge – The Advantages and Dangers

One of the areas that is growing very fast within debiasing and nudging is the concept of advanced analytics and machine learning. This has particularly been used when it comes to identifying talents, behaviours, and future potentials, and is very much used in trying to identify who the great performers are going to be in the future and where they can be found.

Regarding recruitment, there was a global service company that wanted to make the recruitment process more efficient. The way they did this was by acknowledging which type of candidate would automatically go through a round of interviews. This automatically puts forward the top 5 percent of candidates. One of the very positive side effects of this, which wasn't actually planned, was that the number of women that were put through to the first interviews increased massively.

Machine learning is trying to find objective insights using data through advanced statistical algorithms. Unfortunately, somehow those algorithms have to be programmed by humans.

Thus, assumptions come into the algorithms. You also see areas where assumptions are made in the sense that you have missing data. You have to impute numbers where you either put a value to it or an assumption that then gets amplified throughout.

That's why you can—and have to—check very carefully whether your algorithms are working. When we use them in succession planning, for example, or when we use them in recruiting even, we always advise our clients to look back in the past and see whether those algorithms, if they have been used already in recruiting, would have predicted the success of those in their positions right now. So, one has to do a reality check very carefully for every algorithm one puts in place because behind the algorithms are people. That's one very practical example of how to do it.

In merger management, the challenge that a lot of mergers face is that you try to bring together two different corporate cultures and get them to function as one. In that case, there are many biases, especially the in-group and out-group biases that are at play.

But there are also tools—debiasing techniques but also nudging techniques—that can help us prime or create a new common identity. These can be very simple interventions, for example, if you think about how to bring together new teams. What can you do to force the exchange between people who barely know each other?

In traditional management approaches, we tend to assume that money is the biggest motivator—that if you pay your employees more, then they will work more. Now we know that money is actually the hygienic factor. You have to pay them enough, but there are different things that motivate them, like meaningful acknowledgment of the social factor and extrinsic motivation. If it's given for something that in the beginning was not for sale or if it's too low, it can even reduce intrinsic motivation, like enjoyment or self-fulfilment of work. Also, we know that so-called performance-based teams, where you are paid depending on the result of your work, are actually detrimental to creative work because this kind of mindset makes people think narrowly in a particular direction, whereas for creativity you need to think broadly.

Another assumption that you would typically have is that you need to give people honest feedback. You need to tell them what they're doing well, what they're doing not so well, and how to improve it. However, there is a lot of research that shows that people shut off and even try to avoid those from whom they have received such constructive feedback. One of the insights from behavioural economics that a lot of companies are now exploring is to separate developmental feedback from evaluative feedback.

One of the challenges for CEOs and senior executives is that they need to adopt the so-called evidence-management mindset. You need to be ready to test the things that you promote, debiasing algorithms or nudging or anything else, based on large samples of data rather than doing it the way it is usually done—in the past or even today—when a lot of intelligent people get in the room, discuss, and then come out with a decision, which is then rolled out all across the organization.

If we take the example of nudging, it's rather like running an A/B test. You have one group of people who don't get exposed to the nudge and the other group of people who get exposed to the nudge. Then you can measure the difference in behaviour that hopefully occurs between these two groups and also assess the profit impact.

Also, it's still not very intuitive for many companies to think in terms of behaviours. Very often, we think in terms of KPIs (key performance indicators)—for example, customer satisfaction or sales—so it takes some conscious effort to bring it down to the kind of behaviour you're trying to change.

Very often, behaviours are being put into one box together with mindsets, and core businesses are going to be put into a very different box. Putting those boxes together into one and showing how behaviours can be assessed, can be influenced, can be elicited, can be fostered, etc. in the same stringent way as some business processes can be new for many executives.

A lot of people acknowledge that biases have a massive effect on decision-making but don't acknowledge first that they have biases themselves, which is a bias in its own way. That's overconfidence. Even once you've identified a certain bias, you often need some form of external help. For example, in hospitals, they use checklists in order to make sure they don't miss anything and they don't make certain assumptions about things. These are props that can help them overcome some of the biases that they may have or assumptions they make about patients, that are helpful.

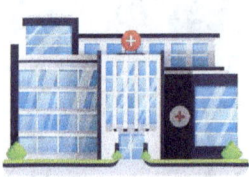

There was some very interesting research in the United States last year that showed the number of mistakes that were made in hospitals between the years 2000 to 2009 in taking people in for accidents and emergencies. There were hundreds and thousands of mistakes being made that they specifically attributed to biases, the main one being "anchoring" and assuming that they've seen the first kind of information that comes, and they stick to that rather than explore any other problems they could have. They estimated that this had an impact of 100,000 lives a year. Being able to save another 100,000 people a year should be motivation enough to try to use these kinds of methodologies.

When you consider international institutions, they're not only starting to deploy those approaches on larger scales but also building their own behavioural-insights unit. They are actively recruiting behavioural psychologists and behavioural economists to work with them.

This takes a few different skills. It takes a deep understanding of analytics and the ability to use data at scale. You need to be able to set up these types of trials and to be able to process them properly. There is an analytical capability that you need to have and build.

Also, you need to have a deep understanding of your business and the opportunity to truly understand the precise behaviour that leads to unwanted outcomes or the precise behaviour that gives you exactly the outcome that you want. So, you need a deep understanding of your business, the way that your people are currently behaving, and the way you would need them to behave in order to fulfil the strategic and organizational goals that you have.

And then you need those that come up with a whole library—and McKinsey has one with over 150 different interventions that are linked to certain nudges that have proved to work in companies in the past. You deploy this database then, to the precise behaviour that you've identified that yields the business outcome. And you use the analytics to track the impact over time. Those are the three main capabilities that you need to build.

Science, Technology, and Leadership

In addition to nudging and positive leadership, a third way that an understanding of human behaviour can have an important impact on business is through behaviour design. Right now, there's a wonderful movement toward more structured approaches to understanding customer experience. There is a focus on the customer journey, on the different points at which a company interacts with the customer—with its products, services, or employees. The aim is to understand the quality of those interactions and improve them. Understanding human behaviour is critical here. For example, if we consider psychology when redesigning the waiting room of a hospital, we can improve the customer experience by providing new and more real-time information to patients or people waiting for family members who are in surgery. We can use sensory marketing techniques to potentially improve the emotional climate in the waiting room. There are many aspects of psychology that we can take into account to help redesign the customer experience.

Understanding positive psychology might help us better understand our own behavioural drivers and make changes in our daily experience to boost our productivity and effectiveness.

Wearable Technology

How is wearable technology going to change the way we work and live?

There's an interesting movement that some people call the "quantified self-movement." It refers to the growing availability and sophistication of wearable devices and sensors—smartwatches, smartphones, chips, and devices we put in our shoes or under our mattress or pillow – that are collecting more and more data on our daily experience, for example, data on our physiological state, sleep movements, or emotional arousal.

This is very interesting because one of the most important drivers of behavioural change is feedback. Typically, in our daily lives, we get very little feedback on ourselves, either from other people or from measurement devices. We may have low blood sugar, but it takes a while for us to realize it. In the interim, when our blood sugar is already very low, we tend to lose the ability to control our behaviour, making us more likely to lose our temper in meetings or get frustrated with someone in a conversation. Having more real-time feedback on our moment-by-moment blood glucose levels could allow us to adapt our behaviour in more productive ways in real time. So that's an example of how this self-measurement movement might shape behaviour in the workplace.

It can also affect our lives in the sense that having feedback on how many steps we're taking each day or on our heart rate variability can allow us to adopt a healthier lifestyle outside of work—which can then help us perform better when we're at work. This data quantification movement is very exciting because it gives us the opportunity to better understand ourselves and the flow of our bodily and emotional states.

As another example, it is also now possible to measure our communications with devices that look like an employee ID badge. These devices can measure the tone and direction of your voice and how often you talk. Today, you can walk out of a meeting and get instant  feedback on your communication style: how much you talked relative to other people, with whom you talked more and less, what tones of voice you used with certain people, and how emotionally aroused you were during a meeting. That's fantastic information that can help us adapt our interpersonal behaviours to be more effective in working in group contexts. We can imagine that when all teams are using these kinds of self-quantification or self-measurement devices, it will provide a great new platform for improving team performance.

Neuroscience and Productivity

How can neuroscience and our understanding of the brain be used to make us more productive in the modern workplace?

There are increasing examples of how neuroscience is starting to inform some of the things happening in the business world and the workplace. Of course, there is neuro-marketing now, where we're starting to  measure how people's brains react to different stimuli and apply that to marketing and consumer behaviour.

How we learn from experience and start to form habits around our behaviours involves a neural system called the mesolimbic dopamine system. Dopamine is a neurotransmitter that has many functions, but one of these important functions relates to a reward-driven neural forecasting system that underlies habit formation.

Habits are automatic behaviours we engage in almost by default, without consciously thinking about doing them. There's a system that develops those habits. When we do a behaviour once, it's obviously not a habit; we do it by choice, and in some contexts, we may have to invest a lot of energy or "willpower" to make it happen (for example, going to the gym on rainy weekend mornings). But once we start repeating a behaviour, and, in particular, once we start repeating it in the same kinds of contexts and situations and receive rewards, a habit starts to form. What we know from neuroscience is that we can think about habits as habit loops or circuits and that they have three components.

The most important component is the actual behaviour, that is, the behavioural routine that makes up the habit. For example, because many people in the modern workplace are busy and are short on time, they interrupt a lot in conversations. They have a habit of interrupting people when they're talking. We could define "interrupting people while they're still talking" as a behavioural routine.

If a particular behaviour is a habit, then there is always something that triggers it: certain situations, a time of day, certain types of people, or certain physiological states. Maybe you are a person who gets frustrated and impatient when you are with someone who tends to be very verbose and provide a lot of detail. You actually feel the frustration in your body; you want to move in your chair. All those things—your frustration, the feeling in your body, this particular person, this kind of context where somebody is talking in great detail—are part of the trigger, or "cue" that sets off your behaviour of interrupting. So now we have two components: what triggers the behaviour and the behaviour itself.

The third component of the habit is the reward. This component has to exist for the habit system to be involved in automating the behaviour. You always get something rewarding for doing a habit-forming behaviour, and that is what makes your brain want to keep doing it. The reward driving habit formation can be getting something positive. For example, when you interrupt somebody, by stopping the person from talking, you might gain a sense of control over the agenda and a sense of renewed efficiency. It can also be rewarding to get rid of something negative. For example, by interrupting someone who is rambling on and on, you end the frustration and impatience that you feel while trying to keep listening. With a habit, there is always a reward.

By understanding these three components, you can train people to analyze unproductive behaviours that they want to change and help them to put in place more positive and productive behaviours. We identify what they do (their routine), why they do it (reward system), and the triggers (cues). Once they understand what drives their current behaviour, we then work to develop a plan for replacing the unproductive behaviour with a more productive one, using along the way a broad range of behavioural tricks to make it easier for that person to make the new desired behaviour more automatic. So that is an example of neuroscience applied in a very concrete way.

There is a behavioural revolution that is starting to have an important impact on the way we organize, develop, and lead people.

Use of Artificial Intelligence in Human Resources Recruitment and Development

Pymetrics, a US-based HR services firm set up by Frida Polli, uses artificial intelligence to assess the suitability of job candidates through a series of techniques. It has some video games that candidates are asked to play. These are designed to assess risk-taking, cooperative teamwork, emotional intelligence, and potential leadership skills.

Large companies also use AI to recruit by short-listing candidates from a set of criteria, thus preventing human bias and making decisions more data-driven. AI also eliminates gender bias, racial bias, and the bias of hailing from famous educational institutions. It also helps to schedule interviews, carry out background checks, monitor productivity, assist in goal setting, help assess performance, recommend training needs, and assess employment satisfaction by trying to increase employee retention or even recommend termination.

According to Kunal Shah (Founder of Cred, an Indian fintech company) in a 2024 article from *The Times of India*, "When Intelligence is Accessible over the Air", efficiency is the largest employer in the world. He points out that whenever large-scale inefficiencies are removed, we witness a revolution. The steam engine minimized inefficiency in transportation, sparking the Industrial Revolution. The internet reduced inefficiencies in information transmission, marking the Digital Revolution. Shah identifies the next major inefficiency as the availability of high-quality intelligence and judgement for everyone. He argues that AI can address this. Just as the internet made information accessible, AI is making intelligence available.

Shah notes that society often relies on scores and resumes to judge creditworthiness, college admissions and job qualifications because it is impractical to evaluate each individual personally. Instead, proxies like degrees, past employers, and alma maters are used. However, he envisions AI revolutionizing this process by replicating the judgement of top experts, allowing for fair, individual assessments. AI could perform in-depth interviews, emulating the decision-making processes of a bank's CRO, a company's CEO, or a college's chief admission officer without relying on traditional methods.

In essence, Shah believes AI will bridge the gaps between talent and opportunity, experts and clients, seekers and sources. As AI augments everyone's thinking, those who execute well – doers and creators – will thrive.

In 2023, AI technical capabilities propelled forward, beating human performance in various benchmarks and improving worker productivity. Yet, the training costs for cutting-edge AI models have soared and there are increased concerns over responsible development and environmental impacts. While this year's descriptor may be acceleration, the authors of the AI Index hope next year we'll also see increasingly diverse expertise contributing to the responsible design, development and study of these systems.

The Good, The Bad, and The Ugly of Big Data AI Algorithms and the Big Boys – Google, Facebook, Amazon, Instagram, Twitter, WhatsApp, and ChatGPT

AI has been about speeding up and supplementing human efforts by accelerating the speed of data assimilation and analysis.

The Google search engine provides fingertip information which otherwise needed visits to libraries, bookstores, educational institutions, and a host of other service providers. These organizations are themselves marketing their own services through Google, Facebook, Amazon, Instagram, Twitter, etc.

Facebook facilitates locating old friends, classmates, and colleagues, and making new friends. It also helps organizations form networks for work, sports, and pleasure. One can photos to keep in touch with loved ones while away at work.

Amazon provides lower-cost products as it has minimized the need for brick-and-mortar buildings and shops, thus providing a cost advantage by being able to ship from large warehouses or get manufacturers to supply directly to customers. Instagram and Twitter provide instant short pictures, ideas, and messages to a large number of people speeding up communications of importance and urgency for people to be alerted about coming storms or other potential calamities.

So far so good, but now a new dimension has emerged through unregulated profit-making monsters that have been unleashed. ChatGPT gives ready answers to any questions asked.

The virtual loss of personal privacy is already upon us with pervasive corporate giants like Google, Facebook and Amazon vested with enormous amounts of personal data of people. The documentary 'Social Dilemma' shows how they are already manoeuvring and controlling peoples' purchasing decisions and relationships by using information from their search engine, search data, prior buying choices, communication, and sharing information via social media. They insidiously send us messages to buy certain products with offers and promotions almost on a real-time basis. Competitors without these advantages are losing out and need to come up with strategies to counter this. Governments are being persuaded to regulate the big boys to create a level playing field. However, it is difficult for them to do so if consumers, while being manipulated, are also getting a price advantage and throwing up alternatives at lightning speed. However, AGI-open general intelligence envisaged by and being developed by Deep Mind and Google Brain (which goes beyond AI in its ability to self-learn and thus have a 'mind of its own', to learn and apply ideas instead of being limited to what it is) is 'fed or programmed' to know how to augment human effort. For instance, if a company wanted to decide to set up a new plant and dedicate a team to figure out locational advantages vis-a-vis land costs, proximity to suppliers, buyers, logistic issues, local laws on taxation, climatic factors, availability of manpower, etc. (a significant task for a project team), AI could accomplish this in minutes, and not the months it might take for a team of humans. It could then issue work orders and set up a monitoring and tracking system to ensure optimum execution of the project.

The emergence of robotics, AI, AGI, and such advanced developments and the convergence of biology and technology, are the issues that will need to be dealt with, with consequences yet unfathomable as these developments could move in any or many directions. So, updated knowledge, scenario-planning, and alternate strategies are the need of the hour for government and corporate leaders.

Companies like Google, Facebook, Microsoft, and Amazon are racing ahead in the area of advanced Artificial Intelligence with projects such as Deep Mind, Google Brain, Facebook AI, and Elon Musk's advanced AI as the cutting-edge technology to stay ahead. It is estimated that advanced AI will add 13 trillion dollars to world economic output, hence being the next arena for competition amongst tech giants.

These companies are now beginning to control human lives by collecting data on every aspect of people's lives and then getting paid by advertisers to pop in front of the audience of whom they have collected the most intimate knowledge by knowing who is where, and who is using Facebook, SMS, WhatsApp, Twitter, Instagram, etc. They can also know from this data, who is sad, happy angry, hungry, thirsty, looking for a job, what kind of job, in a relationship, breaking up from one, who has had a child, is pregnant, every single aspect of all humans who via the internet connect via one of these devices.

The documentary, *The Social Dilemma* contributed to by managers in all the above-mentioned companies brings out how humans are now being manipulated by these companies for profits gained from advertisers who control your mind, the decisions you make, and actions you take.

The constant bombardment with notifications from these companies is becoming addictive to the point of being like a pacifier for babies to quiet them down.

These companies have massive, interconnected computers that speak to each other, also known as machine-learning, where they can create algorithms to figure out the best ad format, colours, shape size, time of day, month, week, etc. for a potential customer who is now a sucker being manipulated to spend time and money on buying, to maximize outcomes for revenue generation for these companies from advertisers. The likes and sharing of photos in every possible action by younger people are creating an obsession to look good, spend money on cosmetics, grooming, and even spend money on surgeries—trends which are now becoming common even amongst young teenagers!

Once set even with the best intentions of the owners of these companies—which is questionable—given that the sole purpose of these algorithms is income and profit generation, they are not in control unless regulations come into place, as have been the case for advertising standards when ads of certain types on radio and print media were regulated for promoting bad health practices—like smoking advertisements, or those on children's channels that promote unhealthy foods.

There has been growing polarisation on account of unbridled fake news about climate change being of no consequence, that one political party was demonic while another angelic, resulting in violence on the streets of countries like the USA, India, and the genocide in countries like Burma. Promoting racial biases through unbridled advertising and posts on gullible people is also rampant. One can post almost anything on social media. Periodically, due to pressures of concerned governments and organizations, some websites, and ad posts of some people or organizations, can be blocked. But this action either comes too late or has too little effect since the algorithms programmed to help these companies continue to do their job very efficiently.

Another lurking danger is that of biases in recruitment and purchases, and racial biases. As an old saying goes, "garbage in garbage out" like in a computer program, the same applies to data analysis by AI and the ensuing algorithms.

For instance, the enormous 'outsourcing' for manufacturing of items like clothing, and IT services in low-cost labour countries of Asia could well be replaced by 3D printers, robots, and artificial intelligence, resulting in unemployment and social unrest in these countries. This could be a boon for developed country leaders but a curse for underdeveloped country leaders, both political and corporate. Corporate leaders would have to explore shutting down some businesses, new areas of business, and alternate training of their employees.

Political leaders are already looking at universal basic income to avoid mass-scale social unrest. But this is easier said than done. Where does the money come from? More taxes on the wealthy? Will they agree? Print more money? Create hyperinflation?

Where Machines Could Replace Humans and Where They Can't

So, here we are finally, at the dawn of the robots. Your organization might now be making use of machine learning and AI to streamline analytics or sharpen customer service. At home, you might no longer have to turn a physical dial to set a kitchen timer or buy groceries—you can yell at Alexa, Siri, or Google to do that hard labour for you. For many of us, that's the extent to which the Fourth Industrial Revolution is affecting us so far. But as computers take over more and more of our tasks, a few of us will see our workplaces untouched by upheaval.

McKinsey (amongst others) has done its best to predict the activities where automation will gain the fastest foothold. Even with *today's* technology—not accounting for near-future advances—it concludes that 60% of all occupations could have at least 30% of their activities automated. It's startling, and it's just the start.

At the same time, with better medical aid and health care knowledge, people are living fitter and longer. So, while job availability is slated to shrink because of robotics taking over many functions, people are living and do not need to retire at 60. They can work and be productive well into their 70s. New young people are entering the workforce, especially in the developing world where the populations are also 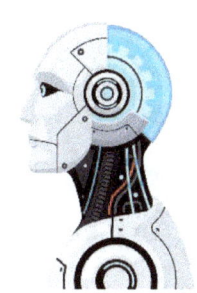 growing. Hence, new social and psychological challenges are in the offing.

That said, some work will be hard to take away from human beings—at least for a while. Back to McKinsey:

"The hardest activities to automate with currently available technologies are those that involve managing and developing people, or that apply expertise to decision making, planning, or creative work."

In other words, we're still uniquely placed to reach deep insight and connection with fellow humans and to display wisdom and innovation in situations where there is no right answer. In a world of automation, we should ensure we're making the most of those distinctly human strengths. But does the average manager know enough about the human mind to be skilled at enabling them? Right now, if they do it at all, most bosses rely on their instincts to create working environments where empathy, wisdom, and creativity can flourish. But behavioural science is increasingly clear and precise on what it takes to do this well. Long-established insights from behavioural economics, psychology, and neuroscience point to scores of small practical tweaks—to the way we run meetings, make decisions, and manage our time—that make it easier for people to function at their cognitive and emotional best. And it wouldn't take much for us to be more deliberate about equipping our up-and-coming leaders with this understanding.

27 LEADERSHIP AND ETHICS

Joanne Ciulla has looked at leadership in the context of basic human nature and instinct. She has examined the issue of self-control and self-interest vs altruism. In the early stages of human history from the time of conquests, and the days of kings and queens, leaders have arisen by inheritance, i.e., being born and not made. Family dynasties, both in politics and business, have been in control, resulting in the self-interest of family, friends, and support groups being a cause of corruption, despotism, and favouritism.

Morality is about right and wrong, while ethics are about virtue and vice. These definitions arise from the teachings of Cicero and Aristotle and have entered the English dictionaries and lexicon. Hence, the debate about leadership has, at its fundamental core, been about values.

Leaders need to be effective and with the support of teams who work with them to deliver results. The question that arises is, are they ethical while being effective? Aristotle used the word *ethios* to talk about morality. The dictionary definition of ethics pertains to morality, and the word *moral* is defined as pertaining to right and wrong, good and evil. It relates to relationships with other people. At times, people try to distinguish between personal morality and ethics as different from the public definition. Leadership researchers like Ciulla and Rost have linked these as a key to the study of leadership, which in the world of business is often ignored or considered adequate if the company fulfils its requirement. Some leaders are effective but not ethical, and some are ethical but not effective.

Typically, ethical behaviour connotes fairness, honesty, respect, compassion, no favouritism, and no racism. Ethical behaviour is reflected in the inclusion of team members, especially in decisions that will affect them, and not simply be dictated to them. Transparency is very important as part of an ethical practice in companies.

For most for-profit corporate organizations, staying within the law of the land is the only requirement of ethical behaviour. Even then, if clever lawyers and accountants find ways around that, it is fine.

Max Bazeman, in his article published in the Harvard Business Review, *A New Model for Ethical Leadership*, says that simplistic ideas of "don't lie, don't cheat", etc. are not adequate, but leaders must embrace a wider view of ideas and actions that are for the benefit of society, not just immediate stakeholders. Leaders must also encompass ethical decisions in the area of hiring and negotiations, and create norms throughout the organization.

Thus, one could view ethical behaviour as being one in which all decisions are taken with a view to benefit all of society.

Perhaps this is a tall order in a cutthroat competitive corporate world where companies battle for resources at the lowest cost to not only maximize profits but also at times to just survive. It would seem that only not-for-profit organizations or governments could fulfil such conditions.

In such circumstances, it becomes to champion the cause of ethical behaviour, highlighting the benefits. Individuals and some organizations are becoming aware of the benefits of ethical behavioural practices.

While there are risks of prosecution for illegal activity, there are but few and far between convictions, due to costly and time-consuming legal processes. Often the benefits of ethical practices are not seen although

recently there have been some legal requirements introduced, such as CSR mandates, investment in the environment, social causes, and others. Young people, like Generation Z and Millennials, are also more conscious of environmental issues and support companies that are conscious of this. Increasingly, investors, business partners, and employees are more inclined to work with ethical companies.

People who are unethical in their personal lives are likely to be unethical in work life as well. One of the justifications for unethical behaviour is that if everyone, especially those at the political level are unethical, then what is the motive for *me* to be ethical?

A New Model for Ethical Leadership

Autonomous vehicles will soon take over the road. While this new technology will save lives by reducing driver error, accidents will still happen. The cars' computers will have to make difficult decisions: when a crash is unavoidable, should the car save its single occupant or five pedestrians? Automobile manufacturers need to tackle such difficult questions in advance and program their cars to respond accordingly. Leaders tasked with answering ethical questions like these should be guided by the goal of creating the most value for society.

Consider two questions posed by the psychologist Daniel Kahneman and colleagues:

How much would you pay to save 2000 migrating birds from drowning in uncovered oil ponds?

How much would you pay to save 200,000 migrating birds from drowning in uncovered oil ponds?

Their research shows that people who are asked the first question offer about the same as do people who are asked the second question. If our goal is to create as much value as possible, a difference in the number of birds should affect how much we choose to pay. This illustrates the limitations of our ethical thinking and suggests that improving ethical decision-making requires rational decisions that maximize value.

The concept of bounded rationality, which is core to the field of behavioural economics, sees managers as wanting to be rational but are influenced by biases and other cognitive limitations. We struggle with bounded ethicality—systematic cognitive barriers that prevent us from being as ethical as we wish to be. By adjusting our personal goals from maximizing benefits for ourselves (and our organizations) to behaving as ethically as possible, we can create more good, increasing well-being for everyone.

Make more of your decisions by comparing options rather than assessing each individually. When we compare multiple options, our decisions are less biased and they create more value. For instance, we donate on the basis of emotional tugs when we consider charities in isolation, but when we make comparisons across charities, we tend to think more about where our contribution will do the most good.

Another strategy involves adapting what the philosopher John Rawls called the *veil of ignorance*. Rawls argued that if you thought about how society should be structured without knowing your status in it (rich or poor, man or woman, etc.)—that is, behind a veil of ignorance—you would make fairer, more ethical decisions. Research shows that those who make ethical decisions behind a veil of ignorance create more value and are more likely to save more lives with scarce resources because they allocate them in less self-interested ways. A related strategy involves removing the social identity of those we judge. Today, companies tend to eliminate names and pictures from applications in an initial hiring review to reduce biased decision-making and increase the odds of hiring the most qualified candidates.

Increasing Your Impact as an Ethical Leader

Leaders can multiply the amount of good they do by encouraging others to be better. People follow the behaviour of others, especially those in positions of power and prestige. By establishing norms for ethical behaviour and empowering employees to help enforce them, leaders can motivate several others to act more ethically themselves.

Leaders can also create more value by shaping the environment in which others make decisions. The most common type of nudge involves changing the default choice that decision-makers face. For instance, a famous nudge encourages organ donation in some European nations by enrolling citizens in the system automatically, letting them opt out if they wish. The program increased the proportion of people agreeing to be donors from less than 30% to more than 80%.

Nine thought leaders were asked to share examples of ethical leadership in the workplace:

Trust Yourself and Your Instincts

"Doing the right thing even when it feels hard or unpopular is the definition of ethical leadership. Even if the people you work with might be upset with a decision you make, trust your instincts, have courage, and think through each decision you make as an ethical leader logically instead of emotionally."
- Dan Reck, MATClinics

Surround Yourself With Other Ethical People

"Ethical leaders have an easier job when they hire ethical employees. Leaders

should seek to maintain a diverse work culture where employees put great importance on company ideals and values while still feeling free to bring different perspectives to the team."
- Ryan Nouis, TruPath

People, Process, and Technology

"First, leaders can get trapped in the smoke and mirrors of "you wouldn't understand, it's technical" used by some vendors and techies to create a smoke and mirrors game that masks core issues with a project. Leaders need to be accountable for every day and dollar regardless of what they are being told. Second, leaders need to make sure that no matter how cool technology may be, it needs to be used, benefit the end-user, and be measured for effectiveness. Technology has tripped up as many leaders as it has catapulted."
- Amy Feind Reeves, JobCoachAmy

Prepare and Rehearse

"Have a clear plan of how you would handle certain ethical scenarios if they were to present themselves. Rehearse the hard conversations, and write down the steps you would like to take depending on the situation. In an ethical crisis, there might not be a lot of time to weigh out your decision. An ethical leader is well prepared and has plans in place for how to handle tough decisions."
- Kimberly Kriewald, AVANA Capital

Requirements Change

"Rather than pushing ahead and demanding terms previously agreed upon are met (which is short-term thinking), the right action may be to end the work for now and re-approach in the future. This gives the client space to focus on what is critical and creates a true partnership for the long term."
- Nicole Spracale, Nicole Spracale Coaching & Consulting

Keep the Basic Human Fundamentals

"People want leaders they can relate to, show and demonstrate legitimate empathy, and not only give clarity on outcomes and goals - but care about their individual goals and outcomes too.

Technology is important, however, these are tools to enhance the fundamentals of being a good leader and human. Ethical leadership is giving people these tools, but not straying away from truly caring and human connection."
- Khabeer Rockley, The 5% Institute

Responsibility Toward the Customer

"Ethical leadership for me is all about putting customers first. It's about training

your team to always do what's right for the customer, no matter what it takes. For example, we have a goal to answer all customer support queries within 12 hours because we've found that this is extremely important for customer retention. That's what ethical leadership is for me - showing the employees that they have a responsibility towards the customer and not their manager."
- Jane Kovalkova, Chanty

Complete Transparency

"One key aspect of ethical leadership is complete transparency. All employees should be kept informed about what the company is doing and how we're getting there, from interns to directors. Transparency fosters trust and goes beyond making promises by actively maintaining constant communication throughout the company."
- Emily Bosak, Markitors

Remind Employees of Their Worth

"It can be easy for a leader to feel the need to smother employees by monitoring their every minute of technology use. With my employees, I have found it a better use of resources to remind them of their worth to the business. I let them know that no one is looking over their shoulder. However, I empower them to own their worth to the entire organization."
- Cade Parian, Parian Injury Law, LLC

REFERENCES

Panchak. P. (2013). *Landmarks in Time: Leadership & Management During the Industrial Revolution [Slideshow],* Industry Week. https://www.industryweek.com/leadership/

World Leaders And Their Leadership Styles History Essay. (2015). UKEssays. https://www.ukessays.com/essays/history/world-leaders-and-their-leadership-styles-history-essay.php

Antonakis, J. (2012). *The Nature of Leadership* (2nd ed.). Sage Publications. https://www.researchgate.net/publication/258221547_Transformational_and_Charismatic_Leadership

Antonakis, J., House, R. J., Rowold, J., & Borgmann, L. (2010). *A fuller full-range leadership theory: Instrumental, transformational, and transactional leadership.* Manuscript submitted for publication.

Bass, B. M., & Riggio, R. E. (2006). *Transformational leadership* (2nd ed.). Mahwah, N.J.: Lawrence Erlbaum.

Bass, B. M. (1985). *Leadership: Good, better, best. Organizational Dynamics,* 13(3), 26–40.

Bass, B. M. (1998). *Transformational leadership: Industrial, military, and educational impact.* Mahwah, NJ: Lawrence Erlbaum.

Bass, B. M. (2008). *The Bass Handbook of Leadership: Theory, Research, and*

Managerial Applications (4th ed.). New York, NY: Free Press.

Bryman, A. (1992) *Charisma and Leadership in Organization.* Sage Publications, London.

Etzioni, A. (1964) *Modern Organizations.* Prentice Hall, Englewood Cliffs.

Fiedler, F. E. (1971). *Validation and extension of the contingency model of leadership effectiveness: A review of empirical findings.* Psychological Bulletin, 76(2), 128–148. https://doi.org/10.1037/h0031454

French, J.R.P. and Raven, B. (1959). *Studies in Social Power, Cartwright, D.* Ann Arbor, MI: Institute for Social Research. http://www.communicationcache.com/uploads/1/0/8/8/108 87248/the_bases_of_social_power_-_chapter_20_-_1959.pdf

Katz, D., & Kahn, R. L. (1978). *The social psychology of organizations.* New York: Wiley.

Liden, R. C., & Antonakis, J. (2009). Considering context in psychological leadership research. Human Relations, 62(11), 1587–1605. https://doi.org/10.1177/0018726709346374

McGrath, J. E. (1962). *New perspectives in organization research :* [consisting of papers from a Conference on Research in Organizations ... June 22 - 24, 1962, a Seminar on the Social Science of Organizations ... June 10 - 23, 1962]. - New York, NY [u.a.] : Wiley. - 1964, p. 533-556.

Schultz, T.W. (1961) *Investment in Human Capital.* American Economic Review, 51, 1-17.

Zaccaro, S. J., Rittman, A. L., & Marks, M. A. (2001). *Team Leadership.* Leadership Quarterly, 12, 451-483. http://dx.doi.org/10.1016/S1048-9843(01)00093-5

Zaleznik, A. (1992/1977). *Managers and leaders: Are they different?* Harvard Business Review, March/April 1992, 70(2), 126-135. First published May/June 1977, 55(3), 67-76.

Heffernan, M. (2014,). *Why Leadership is More Art Than Science.* Inc.com https://www.inc.com/margaret-heffernan/why-leadership-is-more-art-than-science.html

Naseer. T. (2010) *Is Leadership an Art or a Science?* Tanveer Naseer Leadership, https://tanveernaseer.com/is-leadership-an-art-or-a-science/#:~:text=As%20many%20artists%20say%20about,than%20it%20is%20a%20science.

Antonakis, J. & House, R. J. (2002). *Transformational and charismatic leadership: the road ahead.* Amsterdam: JAI.

Balkundi, P., & Kilduff, M. (2005). *The Ties that Lead: A Social Network Approach to Leadership.* The Leadership Quarterly, 16, 941-961. https://doi.org/10.1016/j.leaqua.2005.09.004

Bass, B. M., & Avolio, B. J. (Eds.) (1994). *Improving organizational effectiveness through transformational leadership.* Thousand Oaks, CA: Sage Publications.

Bennis, W., & Nanus, B. (1985). *Leaders: The strategies for taking charge.* New York: Harper & Row.

Blake, R., & Mouton, J. (1964). *The Managerial Grid: The Key to Leadership Excellence.* Houston, TX: Gulf Publishing Company.

Bryman, A. (1992) *Charisma and Leadership in Organization.* Sage Publications, London.

Calder, B. J. (1977). *An Attribution Theory of Leadership.* New Directions in Organizational Behavior, 179, 204.

Conger, J.A. and Kanungo, R.N. (1987) *Toward a Behavioral Theory of Charismatic Leadership in Organizational Settings.* Academy of Management Review, 12, 637-647. https://doi.org/10.5465/amr.1987.4306715

Dansereau, F.J., Graen, G. and Haga, W.J. (1975) *A Vertical Dyad Linkage Approach to Leadership within Formal Organizations: A Longitudinal Investigation of the Role-Making Process.* Organizational Behavior and Human Performance, 13, 46-78.

http://dx.doi.org/10.1016/0030-5073(75)90005-7

Day, D. V., & Lord, R. G. (1988). *Executive leadership and organizational performance: Suggestions for a new theory and methodology.* Journal of Management, 14(3), 453–464.
https://doi.org/10.1177/014920638801400308

Day, D. V., & Zaccaro, S. J. (2007). *Leadership: A Critical Historical Analysis of the Influence of Leader Traits.* In L. L. Koppes (Ed.), Historical perspectives in industrial and organizational psychology (pp. 383–405). Lawrence Erlbaum Associates Publishers.

Barrick, M. R., Day, D. V., Lord, R. G., & Alexander, R. A. (1991). *Assessing the utility of executive leadership.* The Leadership Quarterly, 2(1), 9–22. https://doi.org/10.1016/1048-9843(91)90004-L

Eden, D., & Leviatan, U. (1975). *Implicit Leadership Theory as a Determinant of the Factor Structure Underlying Supervisory Behavior Scales.* Journal of Applied Psychology, 60, 736-741.
http://dx.doi.org/10.1037/0021-9010.60.6.736

Fiedler, F. E. (1993). *The leadership situation and the black box in contingency theories.* In M. M. Chemers & R. Ayman (Eds.), Leadership theory and research: Perspectives and directions (pp. 1–28). Academic Press.

Gardner, W. L., Lowe, K. B., Moss, T. W., Mahoney, K. T., & Cogliser, C. C. (2010). Scholarly leadership of the study of leadership: A review of *The Leadership Quarterly's* second decade, 2000–2009. The Leadership Quarterly, 21(6), 922–958.
https://doi.org/10.1016/j.leaqua.2010.10.003

Gerstner, C. R., &. Day, D. V. (1997). Meta-Analytic Review of *Leader-Member Exchange Theory: Correlates and Construct Issues.* Journal of Applied Psychology, 82, 827-844.
https://doi.org/10.1037/0021-9010.82.6.827

Graen, G.B. and Uhl-Bien, M. (1995) *Relationship-Based Approach to Leadership: Development and Leader-Member Exchange (LMX) Theory of Leadership over 25 Years: Applying a Multi-Level Multi-Domain Perspective.* Leadership Quarterly, 6, 219-247.
http://dx.doi.org/10.1016/1048-9843(95)90036-5

Hater, J. J., & Bass, B. M. (1988). *Superiors' Evaluations and Subordinates' Perceptions of Transformational and Transactional Leadership. Journal of Applied Psychology*, 73, 695-702. http://dx.doi.org/10.1037/0021-9010.73.4.695

House, R. J., & Aditya, R. N. (1997). *The Social Scientific Study of Leadership: Quo Vadis?* Journal of Management, 23, 409-473. http://dx.doi.org/10.1177/014920639702300306

House, R.J., Spangler, W.D. and Woycke, J. (1991) *Personality and Charisma in the US Presidency: A Psychological Theory of Leader Effectiveness.* Academy of Management Journal, 36, 364-396. https://doi.org/10.2307/2393201

House, R.J. (1996). *Path-Goal Theory of Leadership: Lessons, Legacy, and a Reformulated Theory.* The Leadership Quarterly, 7, 323-352. http://dx.doi.org/10.1016/S1048-9843(96)90024-7

Cherry, K. (2023). *'What Is the Great Man Theory of Leadership?',* Very Well Mind. https://www.verywellmind.com/the-great-man-theory-of-leadership-2795311

Cherry, K. (2023). *What Is Autocratic Leadership?* Very Well Mind. https://www.verywellmind.com/what-is-autocratic-leadership-2795314

Cherry, K. (2023). *Is Democratic Leadership the Best Style of Leadership?* Very Well Mind.
https://www.verywellmind.com/what-is-democratic-leadership-2795315

Cherry, K. (2023). *How a Transactional Leadership Style Works.* Very Well Mind.
https://www.verywellmind.com/what-is-transactional-leadership-2795317

Cherry, K. (2023). *Understanding the Trait Theory of Leadership',* Very Well Mind. https://www.verywellmind.com/what-is-the-trait-theory-of-leadership-2795322

Hunt, S.D. (1999). *A general theory of competition: Resources, competences, productivity, economic growth.* Sage Publications

Hunter, J. E., & Schmidt, F. L. (1990). *Methods of meta-analysis: Correcting error and bias in research findings.* Sage Publications, Inc.

Ilies, R., Nahrgang, J.D. and Morgeson, F.P. (2007) *Leader-Member Exchange and Citizenship Behaviors: A Meta-Analysis.* Journal of Applied Psychology, 92, 269-277. https://doi.org/10.1037/0021-9010.92.1.269

Smith, J. E., Carson, K. P., & Alexander, R. A. (1984). *Leadership: It can make a difference.* Academy of Management Journal, 27(4), 765–776. https://doi.org/10.2307/255877

Judge, T. A., Bono, J. E., Ilies, R., & Gerhardt, M. W. (2002). *Personality and leadership: A qualitative and quantitative review.* Journal of Applied Psychology, 87(4), 765–780. https://doi.org/10.1037/0021-9010.87.4.765

Judge, T. A., Piccolo, R. F., & Ilies, R. (2004). *The Forgotten Ones? The Validity of Consideration and Initiating Structure in Leadership Research.* The Journal of Applied Psychology, 89, 36-51. http://dx.doi.org/10.1037/0021-9010.89.1.36

Katz, D., Maccoby, N., Gurin, G., & Floor, L. G. (1951). *Productivity, supervision and morale among railroad workers.* Survey Research Center, Institute f.

Lord, R. G., & Emrich, C. G. (2000). *Thinking outside the box by looking inside the box: Extending the cognitive revolution in leadership research.* The Leadership Quarterly, 11(4), 551–579. https://doi.org/10.1016/S1048-9843(00)00060-6

Lord, R. G., & Maher, K. J. (1991). *Leadership and Information Processing:, Linking Perceptions and Performance.* Academy of Management Review, 18, 153.

Lord, R. G., Binning, J. F., Rush, M. C., & Thomas, J. C. (1978). *The effect of performance cues and leader behavior on questionnaire ratings of leadership behavior.* Organizational Behavior & Human Performance, 21(1),

27–39. https://doi.org/10.1016/0030-5073(78)90036-3

Lord, R. G., Brown, D. J., Harvey, J. L., & Hall, R. J. (2001). *Contextual constraints on prototype generation and their multilevel consequences for leadership perceptions.* The Leadership Quarterly, 12(3), 311–338. https://doi.org/10.1016/S1048-9843(01)00081-9

Lord, R. G., De Vader, C. L., & Alliger, G. M. (1986). *A Meta-Analysis of the Relation between Personality Traits and Leadership Perceptions: Procedures.* Journal of Applied Psychology, 71, 402-410.

Lord, R. G., Foti, R. J., & De Vader, C. L. (1984). *A Test of Leadership Categorization Theory: Internal Structure, Information Processing, and Leadership Perception.* Organizational Behavior and Human Performance, 34, 343-378. https://doi.org/10.1016/0030-5073(84)90043-6

Lowe, K. B. & Gardner, B. (2000) *Ten years of Leadership Quarterly: Contributions and challenges for the future.* The Leadership Quarterly, 11(4), 1-56.

Mann, R. D. (1959). *A Review of the Relationship between Personality and Performance in Small Groups.* Psychological Bulletin, 66, 241-27 http://dx.doi.org/10.1037/h0044587

Meindl, J. R., & Ehrlich, S. B. (1987). *The romance of leadership and the evaluation of organizational performance.* Academy of Management Journal, 30(1), 91–109. https://doi.org/10.2307/255897

Meindl, J. R., Ehrlich, S. B., & Dukerich, J. M. (1985). *The romance of leadership.* Administrative Science Quarterly, 30(1), 78–102. https://doi.org/10.2307/2392813

Salancik, G.R. and Pfeffer, J. (1977) An Examination of Need-Satisfaction Models of Job Attitudes. Administrative Science Quarterly, 22, 427-456. https://doi.org/10.2307/2392182

Rush, M. C., Thomas, J. C., & Lord, R. G. (1977). Implicit leadership theory: A potential threat to the internal validity of leader behavior questionnaires. Organizational Behavior & Human Performance, 20(1), 93–110. https://doi.org/10.1016/0030-

5073(77)90046-0

Stogdill, R. M., & Coons, A. E. (Eds.). (1957). *Leader behavior: Its description and measurement.* Ohio State Univer., Bureau of Busin.

Stogdill, R. (1948). *Personal Factors Associated with Leadership: A Survey of the Literature.* Journal of Psychology, 25, 35-71. https://doi.org/10.1080/00223980.1948.9917362

Van Seters, D., & Field, R. (1990). *The Evolution of Leadership Theory.* Journal of Organizational Change Management, 3, 29-45. https://doi.org/10.1108/09534819010142139

Vroom, V. H., & Jago, A. G. (1988). *The new leadership: Managing participation in organizations.* Prentice-Hall, Inc.

Vroom, V., & Yetton, P. (1973). *Leadership and Decision-Making.* Pittsburgh, PA: University of Pittsburgh Press. https://doi.org/10.2307/j.ctt6wrc8r

Wofford, J. C., Goodwin, V. L., & Whittington, J. L. (1998). *A field study of a cognitive approach to understanding transformational and transactional leadership.* The Leadership Quarterly, 9(1), 55–84. https://doi.org/10.1016/S1048-9843(98)90042-X

Zaccaro, S. J., Dubrow, S., & Kolze, M. (2018). *Leader traits and attributes.* In J. Antonakis & D. V. Day (Eds.), *The nature of leadership* (3rd ed., pp. 29–55). Sage Publications, Inc. https://doi.org/10.4135/9781506395029.n2

Fiori, M., & Antonakis, J. (2011). *The ability model of emotional intelligence: Searching for valid measures.* Personality and Individual Differences, 50(3), 329–334. https://doi.org/10.1016/j.paid.2010.10.010

Antonakis, J., Avolio, B.J. and Sivasubramaniam, N. (2003). *Context and Leadership: An Examination of the Nine-Factor Full-Range Leadership Theory Using the Multifactor Leadership Questionnaire.* The Leadership Quarterly, 14, 261-295. https://doi.org/10.1016/S1048-9843(03)00030-4

Bass, B. M., & Steidlmeier, P. (1999). *Ethics, Character, and Authentic Transformational Leadership Behavior.* The Leadership Quarterly, 10, 181-217.
https://doi.org/10.1016/S1048-9843(99)00016-8

Brown, M. E., & Treviño, L. K. (2006). Ethical Leadership: *A Review and Future Directions.* The Leadership Quarterly, 17, 595-616.
https://doi.org/10.1016/j.leaqua.2006.10.004

Day, D. V., Harrison, M. M., & Halpin, S. M. (2009). *An integrative approach to leader development: Connecting adult development, identity and expertise.* Routledge/Taylor & Francis Group.

Deluga, R. J. (1990). *The Effects of Transformational, Transactional, and Laissez Faire Leadership Characteristics on Subordinate Influencing Behavior.* Basic and Applied Social Psychology, 11, 191-203.
https://doi.org/10.1207/s15324834basp1102_6

Eagly, A. H., & Carli, L. L. (2007). *Through the labyrinth: The truth about how women become leaders.* Harvard Business School Press.

Eagly, A. H., & Chin, J. L. (2010). *Diversity and leadership in a changing world.* American Psychologist, 65, 216-224. doi:10.1037/a0018957

Gerstner, C.R. and Day, D.V. (1997) *Meta-Analytic Review of Leader Member Exchange Theory: Correlates and Construct Issues.* Journal of Applied Psychology, 82, 827-844.
http://dx.doi.org/10.1037/0021-9010.82.6.827

Hannah, S. T., Uhl-Bien, M., Avolio, B. J., & Cavarretta, F. L. (2009). *A framework for examining leadership in extreme contexts.* The Leadership Quarterly, 20(6), 897–919.
https://doi.org/10.1016/j.leaqua.2009.09.006

House, R. J., Hanges, P. J., Javidan, M., Dorfman, P. W., & Gupta, V. (2004). *Culture, Leadership, and Organizations: The GLOBE Study of 62 Societies.* Thousand Oaks, CA: Sage Publications.

Howell, J. M., & Hall-Merenda, K. E. (1999). *The ties that bind: The impact of leader-member exchange, transformational and transactional leadership, and distance on predicting follower performance.* Journal of Applied

Psychology, 84(5), 680–694. https://doi.org/10.1037/0021-9010.84.5.680

Livers, A., & Caver. K. (2003). *Leading in Black and White: Working Across the Racial Divide in Corporate America.* Wiley, 2003.

Osborn, R. N., & Marion, R. (2009). *Contextual leadership, transformational leadership and the performance of international innovation seeking alliances.* The Leadership Quarterly, 20(2), 191–206. https://doi.org/10.1016/j.leaqua.2009.01.010

Porter, L. W., & McLaughlin, G. B. (2006). *Leadership and the Organizational Context: Like the Weather?* The Leadership Quarterly, 17, 559-576. http://dx.doi.org/10.1016/j.leaqua.2006.10.002

Howell, J.M. and Shamir, B. (1999). *Organizational and Contextual Influences on the Emergence and Effectiveness of Charismatic Leadership.* The Leadership Quarterly, 10, 257-283. https://doi.org/10.1016/S1048-9843(99)00014-4

Turner, N., Barling, J., Epitropaki, O., Butcher, V. and Milner, C. (2002). *Transformational Leadership and Moral Reasoning.* Journal of Applied Psychology, 87, 304-311. http://dx.doi.org/10.1037/0021-9010.87.2.304

Goldsmith. M., & Mulally. A. (n.d.) *The Leader as the Facilitator: How to Effectively Lead Knowledge Workers.* Training Industry Magazine https://trainingindustry.com/magazine/issue/the-leader-as-the-facilitator-how-to-effectively-lead-knowledge-workers/

Davis. S. (2011). *Facilitation as a Leadership Style.* FacilitatorU.com https://facilitatoru.com/facilitation/facilitation-as-a-leadership-style/

Martinuzzi. B. (2023). *7 Leadership Styles and How to Find Your Own.* American Express. https://www.americanexpress.com/en-us/business/trends-and-insights/articles/the-7-most-common-leadership-styles-and-how-to-find-your-own/

Indeed Editorial Team (2023). *10 Common Leadership Styles.* Indeed.com. https://in.indeed.com/career-advice/career-development/10-common-leadership-styles

Bachrach, P., & A. Botwink. (1992). *Power and Empowerment: A Radical Theory of Participatory Democracy.* Philadelphia: Temple University Press.

Bass, B. (1996). *A New Paradigm of Leadership: An Inquiry into Transformational Leadership.* Alexandria VA: U.S. Army Research Institute for the Behavioral and Social Sciences.

Burns, J. M. (1978). *Leadership.* New York: Harper and Row.

Corning, P. (1984). T*he Synergism Hypothesis: A Theory of Progressive Evolution.* New York: McGraw-Hill.

Deutsch, K. (1980). *Politics and Government: How People Decide their Fate.* Boston: Houghton-Mifflin.

Easton, D. (1971). *The Political System: An Inquiry into the State of Political Science.* 2d ed. New York: Knopf.

Foucault, M. (1980). *Power/Knowledge: Selected Interviews and Other Writings,* 1972-79, (Ed. Colin Gordon). New York: Pantheon.

Hackman, M., & C. Johnson. (1996). *Leadership: A Communication Perspective.* 2d ed. Prospect Heights, IL: Waveland Press.

Janda, K. (1960). *Towards the Explication of the Concept of Leadership in Terms of the Concept of Power.* Human Relations 13:345u63.

Leftwinch, A., ed. (1990). *New Developments in Political Science.* Brookfield, VT: Gower Publishing Co.

Mughan, A, & S. Patterson. (1992). *Political Leadership in Democratic Societies.* Chicago: Nelson Hall.

Murrell, K. (1997). *Emergent Theories of Leadership for the Next Century: Towards Relational Concepts.* Organization Development Journal 15 (3):35-42.

Robertson, P., & S. Tang. (1995). *The Role of Commitment in Collective Action: Comparing the Organizational Behavior and Rational Choice Perspectives.* Public Administration Review. 55:67-80.

Stogdill, R. (1950). *Leadership, Membership, and Organization.* Psychological Bulletin 47:1-4

Tucker, R. (1981). *Politics as Leadership.* Columbia, MO: University of Missouri Press.

Verba, S. (1961). *Small Groups and Political Behavior: A Study of Leadership.* Princeton, NJ: Princeton University Press.

Weaver, D. (1991). *Liberalism and Leadership: Lockean Roots.* Leadership Quarterly 2(3): 157-74.

Welsh, W. (1979). *Leaders and Elites.* New York: Holt, Rinehart and Winston.

Wilson, R., & C. Rhodes. (1997). *Leadership and Credibility in N-Person Coordination Games.* Journal of Conflict Resolution 41(6): 767-91.

Yuki, G. (1998.) *Leadership in Organizations.* 4th ed. Upper Saddle River, NJ: Prentice Hall.

Krow, E. (2017). *The Key to Employee–Empowering Leadership.* Forbes. https://www.forbes.com/sites/forbescoachescouncil/2017/06/14/the-key-to-employee-empowering-leadership/?sh=4b6959101267

Brower, H.H., Lester. S.W., & Korsgaard. M.A. (2017). *Want Your Employees to Trust You? Show You Trust Them.* Harvard Business Review.
https://hbr.org/2017/07/want-your-employees-to-trust-you-show-you-trust-them

Hopkin, M. R. (2013). *Why leaders need a long term vision.* Lead on Purpose. https://leadonpurposeblog.com/2013/12/27/why-leaders-need-a-long-term-vision/

Anderson, Erika. (2012). *Passionate Leaders Aren't Loud – They're Deep.* Forbes.

https://www.forbes.com/sites/erikaandersen/2012/06/11/passionate-leaders-arent-loud-theyre-deep/?sh=63c74052182c

Kay, M. (n.d.) *Leadership Skills #2: Great Leaders Ignite Passion. AboutLeaders.* https://aboutleaders.com/leadership-skills-2-great-leaders-ignite-passion/

5 Key Traits of Great Leaders. (2006). Entrepreneur. https://www.entrepreneur.com/leadership/5-key-traits-of-great-leaders/163590

Morgan, N. (2015). *The Art of Passionate Leadership.* Forbes. https://www.forbes.com/sites/ellevate/2015/07/08/the-art-of-passionate-leadership/?sh=17dbc99d4484

Mind Tools Content Team. (n.d.). *Building Good Work Relationships.* MindTools. https://www.mindtools.com/aorqe4z/building-good-work-relationships

How to Build Good Relationships with Project Stakeholders. (n.d.) Portfolio Manager. https://www.liquidplanner.com/blog/build-good-relationships-project-stakeholders/

Schaefer, B. (2015). *On Becoming a Leader: Building Relationships and Creating Communities.* Educause Review. https://er.educause.edu/articles/2015/10/on-becoming-a-leader-building-relationships-and-creating-communities

Rapp, K. (2014). Have You Told Them Lately That You Love Them? Inc.
https://www.inc.com/kathy-rapp/leadership-strategies-relationship-building.html

Hopkin, M. R. (2011). *Leadership is a Relationship.* Lead on Purpose. https://leadonpurposeblog.com/2011/11/26/leadership-is-a-relationship/

Hemerling, J. (n.d.). *5 Ways to Deal in an Era of Constant Change.* T-Three.com. https://www.t-three.com/videos-blog/5-ways-to-lead-in-an-era-of-constant-change

Sinek, S. (2009) *How Great Leaders Inspire Action.* Ted.com. https://www.ted.com/talks/simon_sinek_how_great_leaders_inspire_action?language=en#t-662480

Amiss, H. (2016). *How to Establish Authenticity in Leadership: Trust, Feedback, Change.* T-Three.com. https://www.t-three.com/soak/insights/how-to-establish-authenticity-in-leadership-trust-feedback-change

Torgovnick, K. (2012). 5 *Insights from Brene Brown's New Book, Daring Greatly, Out Today.* Ted Blog. https://blog.ted.com/5-insights-from-brene-browns-new-book-daring-greatly-out-today/

McDowell, T., Rahnema, A., & Van Durme, Y. (2017). *The Organizations of the Future: Arriving now.* Deloitte Insights. https://www2.deloitte.com/insights/us/en/focus/human-capital-trends/2017/organization-of-the-future.html

Seijts, G. (2013). *Good Leaders Never Stop Learning.* Ivey Business Journal. https://iveybusinessjournal.com/publication/good-leaders-never-stop-learning/

Mikkelsen, K., & Jarche, H. (2015). *The Best Leaders are Constant Learners.* Harvard Business Review. https://hbr.org/2015/10/the-best-leaders-are-constant-learners

Zenger, J., & Folkman, J. (2014). *Your Employees Want the Negative Feedback You Hate to Give.* Harvard Business Review. https://hbr.org/2014/01/your-employees-want-the-negative-feedback-you-hate-to-give

Kluger, A.N. and DeNisi, A. (1996) *The Effects of Feedback Interventions on Performance: A Historical Review, a Meta-Analysis, and a Preliminary Feedback Intervention Theory.* Psychological Bulletin, 119, 254-284. http://dx.doi.org/10.1037/0033-2909.119.2.254

Nowack, K.M. (2014). *Take the Sting Out of Feedback.* T.D. Magazine. https://www.td.org/magazines/td-magazine/take-the-sting-out-of-feedback

Developing an Open Feedback Culture. (n.d.). T-Three.com. https://www.t-three.com/developing-an-open-feedback-culture

Mulder, P. (n.d.). *Management by Objectives (MBO).* Toolshero.com. https://www.toolshero.com/management/management-by-objectives-drucker/

Farmiloe, B. (2024). *9 Examples of Ethical Leadership in the Workplace.* https://www.score.org/resource/blog-post/9-examples-ethical-leadership-workplace

Bazerman, M.H. (2020). *A New Model for Ethical Leadership.* Harvard Business Review. https://hbr.org/2020/09/a-new-model-for-ethical-leadership

Antonakis, John & Dalgas, Olaf. (2009). *Predicting Elections: Child's Play!.* Science (New York, N.Y.). 323. 1183. 10.1126/science.1167748.

Antonakis, J., Ashkanasy, N. M., & Dasborough, M. T. (2009). *Does leadership need emotional intelligence?* The Leadership Quarterly, 20(2), 247–261. https://doi.org/10.1016/j.leaqua.2009.01.006

Arvey, R. D., Rotundo, M., Johnson, W., Zhang, Z., & McGue, M. (2006). *The determinants of leadership role occupancy: Genetic and personality factors.* The Leadership Quarterly, 17(1), 1–20. https://doi.org/10.1016/j.leaqua.2005.10.009

Arvey, Richard & Zhang, Zhen & Avolio, Bruce & Krueger, Robert. (2007). *Developmental and Genetic Determinants of Leadership Role Occupancy among Females.* The Journal of applied psychology. 92. 693-706. 10.1037/0021-9010.92.3.693.

Caldu, Xavier & Dreher, Jean-Claude. (2007). Caldu X, Dreher JC. *Hormonal and genetic influences on processing reward and social information.* Ann N Y Acad Sci 1118: 43-73. Annals of the New York Academy of Sciences. 1118. 43-73. 10.1196/annals.1412.007.

Chiao, Joan & Mathur, Vani & Harada, Tokiko & Lipke, Trixie. (2009). *Neural Basis of Preference for Human Social Hierarchy versus Egalitarianism.* Annals of the New York Academy of Sciences. 1167. 174-81. 10.1111/j.1749-6632.2009.04508.x.

Grant, V. J., & France, J. T. (2001). *Dominance and testosterone in women.* Biological Psychology, 58(1), 41–47. https://doi.org/10.1016/S0301-0511(01)00100-4

Gray, Noella & Campbell, Lisa. (2007). *A Decommodified Experience? Exploring Aesthetic, Economic, and Ethical Values for Volunteer Ecotourism in Costa Rica.* Journal of Sustainable Tourism. 15. 463-482. 10.2167/jost725.0.

Judge, T. A., & Ilies, R. (2004). *Affect and Job Satisfaction: A Study of Their Relationship at Work and at Home.* Journal of Applied Psychology, 89(4), 661–673. https://doi.org/10.1037/0021-9010.89.4.661

Ilies, R., Gerhardt, M. W., & Le, H. (2004). *Individual Differences in Leadership Emergence: Integrating Meta-Analytic Findings and Behavioral Genetics Estimates.* International Journal of Selection and Assessment, 12(3), 207–219. https://doi.org/10.1111/j.0965-075X.2004.00275.x

Smith, K. B., Larimer, C. W., Littvay, L., & Hibbing, J. R. (2007). *Evolutionary theory and political leadership: Why certain people do not trust decision makers.* The Journal of Politics, 69(2), 285–299. https://doi.org/10.1111/j.1468-2508.2007.00532.x

Kramer, R. S. S., Arend, I., & Ward, R. (2010). *Perceived health from biological motion predicts voting behaviour.* The Quarterly Journal of Experimental Psychology, 63(4), 625–632. https://doi.org/10.1080/17470210903490977

Sellers, J. G., Mehl, M. R., & Josephs, R. A. (2007). *Hormones and personality: Testosterone as a marker of individual differences.* Journal of Research in Personality, 41(1), 126–138. https://doi.org/10.1016/j.jrp.2006.02.004

Van Vugt, M., & Schaller, M. (2008). *Evolutionary approaches to group dynamics: An introduction.* Group Dynamics: Theory, Research, and Practice, 12(1), 1–6. https://doi.org/10.1037/1089-2699.12.1.1

Villarejo-Galende, Alberto & Puertas-Martín, Verónica & Moreno-Ramos, Teresa & Camacho-Salas, Ana & Porta-Etessam, Jesús &

Bermejo-Pareja, Félix. (2011). *Mirrored-self misidentification in a patient without dementia: Evidence for right hemispheric and bifrontal damage.* Neurocase. 17. 276-84. 10.1080/13554794.2010.498427.

Cohen, H. (2020). *A Political Leader.* Leadership Expert. https://www.leadershipexpert.co.uk/political-leader.html

Beard, A. (2014) *Leading with Humor.* Harvard Business Review. https://hbr.org/2014/05/leading-with-humor

Why Workplace Humour is the Secret to Great Leadership. (2018). Rise. https://risepeople.com/blog/why-workplace-humour-is-the-secret-to-great-leadership/

Pourbahrami, V. (n.d.) *Why Top Leaders Use Humor in Their Leadership Skills – Humor That Works.* Humor That Works. https://www.humorthatworks.com/benefits/why-leaders-use-humor-at-work/

Howard, J. (2018). *Why Work Life Balance is Important for Leaders.* LinkedIn. https://www.linkedin.com/pulse/why-work-life-balance-important-leaders-jo-howard/

Feiste, G. (2011). *A Balanced Life – Does It Make For a Better Leader?* Lead Change Group. https://leadchangegroup.com/a-balanced-life-does-it-make-for-a-better-leader/

Kehl, T. (2012). *12 Key Strategies to Achieving a Work-Life Balance.* Industry Week. https://www.industryweek.com/leadership/article/21982458/12-key-strategies-to-achieving-a-worklife-balance

Comaford, C. (2018). *3 Daily Actions That Guarantee Work-Life Balance For Leaders.* Forbes. https://www.forbes.com/sites/christinecomaford/2018/02/24/3-daily-actions-that-guarantee-work-life-balance-for-leaders/?sh=7e00a2684ee5

Hargreaves, N. (2019). *Common Reasons Leaders Fail.* LinkedIn. https://www.linkedin.com/pulse/21-common-reasons-leaders-fail-nick-hargreaves/

Sommer, T. (2018). *Leadership Animals: An Introduction.* The Medium. https://medium.com/redbubble/leadership-spirit-animals-introduction-6c5c35874cf

Kouzes, J. M., & Posner, B. Z. (1987). *The Leadership Challenge: How to Get Extraordinary Things Done in Organizations (1st ed.).* San Francisco: Jossey-Bass.

Newstron, J. W., & Davis, K. (1993). *Organizational behaviour, human behaviour at work.* New York: McGraw-Hill.

Ivancevich, J., Konopaske, R., & Matteson, M. (2007). Organizational Behavior and Management. McGraw-Hill Irwin.

Haslam, S. A., & Reicher, S. D. (2016). *Rethinking the Psychology of Leadership: From Personal Identity to Social Identity.* Daedelus, Journal of the American Academy of Arts and Sciences, 145, 21-34. https://doi.org/10.1162/DAED_a_00394

Harris, H. (2017). *Lemonade is Using Behavioural Science to Onboard Customers and Keep them Honest.* Fast Company. https://www.fastcompany.com/3068506/lemonade-is-using-behavioural-science-to-onboard-customers-and-keep-them-honest

Measuring a Company's Entire Social and Environmental Impact. (n.d.) B Corporation. https://bcorporation.net/about-b-corps

Uber Press Team. (2017). *Remarks from Uber Press Call.* Uber Newsroom.

https://www.uber.com/newsroom/press-call

https://www.lemonade.com/blog/

http://www.insurtechventure.com/

https://www.nytimes.com/by/noam-scheiber

Kuhlen, A. (2017). *Overcoming New Nonprofit Challenges through Leadership*

Investment. The Center for Effective Philanthropy. https://cep.org/overcoming-new-nonprofit-challenges-leadership-investment/

Oesch, T. (2019). *Leadership Development for the Fourth Industrial Revolution. Training Industry.* https://trainingindustry.com/articles/leadership/leadership-development-for-the-fourth-industrial-revolution/

Bawany, S. (n.d.). *Future Of Leadership In The Fourth Industrial Revolution.* Strategic Leadership. https://strategicleaders.com/future-leadership-fourth-industrial-revolution/

Raffoni, M. (2020). *5 Questions that Newly Virtual Leaders Should Ask Themselves.* Harvard Business Review. https://hbr.org/2020/05/5-questions-that-newly-virtual-leaders-should-ask-themselves

Brüggemann, P., Güntner, A., Lorenz J.T., & Münstermann, B. (2017). *A Nudge for the Better In Assistance Claims Journeys.* McKinsey & Company. https://www.mckinsey.com/industries/financial-services/our-insights/a-nudge-for-the-better-in-assistance-claims-journeys

Hoffman, N., Huber, M., & Smith, M. (2017). *An Analytics Approach to Debiasing Asset Management Decisions.* McKinsey & Company. https://www.mckinsey.com/industries/financial-services/our-insights/an-analytics-approach-to-debiasing-asset-management-decisions

Günther, B., Heiligtag, S., & Webb, A. (2017). *A Case Study in Combating Bias.* McKinsey & Company. https://www.mckinsey.com/capabilities/people-and-organizational-performance/our-insights/a-case-study-in-combating-bias

Baer, T., & Kamalnath, V. (2017). Controlling Machine Learning Algorithms and their Biases. McKinsey & Company. https://www.mckinsey.com/business-functions/risk/our-insights/controlling-machine-learning-algorithms-and-their-biases

Meissner, P., Sibony, O., & Wulf, T. (2015). Are You Ready to Decide? McKinsey & Company. https://www.mckinsey.com/capabilities/strategy-and-corporate-finance/our-insights/are-you-ready-to-decide

Chui, M., Manyika, J., & Miremadi, M. (2016). *Where Machines Could Replace Humans and Where They Can't Yet.* McKinsey & Company. https://www.mckinsey.com/business-functions/mckinsey-digital/our-insights/where-machines-could-replace-humans-and-where-they-cant-yet

Arnsten, Amy. (2009). *Stress signaling pathways that impair prefrontal cortex structure and function.* Nature reviews. Neuroscience. 10. 410-22. 10.1038/nrn2648.

Arnsten, Amy. (2009). *Stress signaling pathways that impair prefrontal cortex structure and function.* Nature reviews. Neuroscience. 10. 410-22. 10.1038/nrn2648.

Mann, A., & Harter, J. (2016). *The Worldwide Employee Engagement Crisis.* Gallup. https://www.gallup.com/workplace/236495/worldwide-employee-engagement-crisis.aspx

Kang, Min & Hsu, Ming & Krajbich, Ian & Loewenstein, George & McClure, Samuel M. & Wang, Joseph & Camerer, Colin. (2009). *The Wick in the Candle of Learning: Epistemic Curiosity Activates Reward Circuitry and Enhances Memory.* Psychological science. 20. 963-73. 10.1111/j.1467-9280.2009.02402.x.

Di Stefano, Giada and Gino, Francesca and Pisano, Gary and Staats, Bradley R., Learning by Thinking: *How Reflection Can Spur Progress Along the Learning Curve* (February 6, 2023). Harvard Business School NOM Unit Working Paper No. 14-093, Kenan Institute of Private Enterprise Research Paper No. 2414478, Available at SSRN: https://ssrn.com/abstract=2414478 or http://dx.doi.org/10.2139/ssrn.2414478

Friedman, R., Deci, E.L., Elliot, A.J. et al. Motivational synchronicity: Priming motivational orientations with observations of others' behaviors. Motiv Emot 34, 34–38 (2010). https://doi.org/10.1007/s11031-009-9151-3

Wild, B., Erb, M., & Bartels, M. (2001). Are emotions contagious? Evoked emotions while viewing emotionally expressive faces: Quality, quantity, time course and gender differences. Psychiatry Research, 102(2), 109–124. https://doi.org/10.1016/S0165-1781(01)00225-6

Quartz Daily Brief. https://qz.com/emails/daily-brief/

Chancellor J, Margolis S, Jacobs Bao K, Lyubomirsky S. Everyday prosociality in the workplace: The reinforcing benefits of giving, getting, and glimpsing. Emotion. 2018 Jun;18(4):507-517. doi: 10.1037/emo0000321. Epub 2017 Jun 5. PMID: 28581323.

Neumann, C. S., & Hare, R. D. (2008). Psychopathic traits in a large community sample: Links to violence, alcohol use, and intelligence. Journal of Consulting and Clinical Psychology, 76(5), 893–899. https://doi.org/10.1037/0022-006X.76.5.893

About the Author

Dr. Hiru Bijlani is a leadership guru, holding a Doctorate in Business Policy and Administration, besides an Honours Bachelor's Degree in Science and a Masters' Diploma in Advanced Business.

He has over 30 years management and consulting experience in diverse organizations in India, USA, Europe, Africa, the Gulf, and Southeast Asian countries.

He is the author of numerous articles and seven books, namely *Globalization – an Overview*, and *A Guide to Global Joint Ventures and Alliances*, both published by Heinemann Asia, Singapore and *Succeed in Business: India*, and *Tips and Tales for Travelers* published by Times Edition Pte Ltd, Singapore, *Success Yogi – Your Guru for Success and Happiness*, *Roadmap to Success and Happiness*, and his latest book, *Leadership: Past, Present & Future*. Some of these books have been translated and published in other international languages.

He is the former President of the Institute of Management Consultants of India, the apex body of the management consulting profession in India. He has played various roles in other professional, business and government bodies and institutions, such as The Indo-American Chamber of Commerce, The Government of India MOU Committee for Public Sector Enterprises, etc.

He has participated in global conferences like the meetings of the International Council of Management Consulting Institutes, World Economic Forum Davos, and other conferences in Asia, Europe, Latin America and the USA. Recently, he was a resource person at *Building a Better Asia* Future Leader's Dialogue at Beijing.

He is the Advisor of Leadership Management International in South Asia. His email id is hirubijlani@gmail.com

www.ingramcontent.com/pod-product-compliance
Lightning Source LLC
Chambersburg PA
CBHW071828210526
45479CB00001B/43